WONDER WOMAN

+ VOLUME.2 +

THROUGH A GLASS DARKLY

+ VOLUME.2 +

THROUGH A GLASS DARKLY

BECKY CLOONAN, MICHAEL W. CONRAD
WRITERS

MARCIO TAKARA, ANDY MacDONALD, TRAVIS G. MOORE, JIM CHEUNG, STEVE PUGH
ARTISTS

TAMRA BONVILLAIN, NICK FILARDI, MARCELO MAIOLO
COLORISTS

PAT BROSSEAU
LETTERER

TRAVIS G. MOORE AND TAMRA BONVILLAIN
COLLECTION COVER ARTISTS

Brittany Holzherr	Editor – Original Series & Collected Edition
Chris Rosa	Associate Editor – Original Series
Bixie Mathieu	Assistant Editor – Original Series
Steve Cook	Design Director – Books & Publication Design
Suzannah Rowntree	Publication Production
Marie Javins	Editor-in-Chief, DC Comics
Anne DePies	Senior VP – General Manager
Jim Lee	Publisher & Chief Creative Officer
Don Falletti	VP – Manufacturing Operations & Workflow Management
Lawrence Ganem	VP – Talent Services
Alison Gill	Senior VP – Manufacturing & Operations
Jeffrey Kaufman	VP – Editorial Strategy & Programming
Nick J. Napolitano	VP – Manufacturing Administration & Design
Nancy Spears	VP – Revenue

WONDER WOMAN VOL. 2: THROUGH A GLASS DARKLY

DC Comics, 2900 West Alameda Ave., Burbank, CA 91505
Printed by Solisco Printers, Scott, QC, Canada. 7/8/22. First Printing.
ISBN: 978-1-77951-660-2

Library of Congress Cataloging-in-Publication Data is available.

STEVE TREVOR'S APARTMENT.
WASHINGTON, D.C.
2:54 A.M.
DON'T WORRY ABOUT THOSE, ETTA, I'LL GET 'EM IN THE MORNING.
WILL YOU THOUGH? I SUSPECT YOU'LL BE MOVING PRETTY SLOW TOMORROW.

WELL...I APPRECIATE YOU VERY MUCH, MS. CANDY.
I DON'T KNOW WHAT I'D DO WITHOUT YOU, ESPECIALLY OVER THESE PAST FEW MONTHS.
PLEASE. ALL I DO IS KEEP YOU BUSY.
IT'S BEEN A WHILE SINCE YOU'VE HAD FRIENDS OVER. WAS IT GOOD TO SEE 'EM?
CHIPPY CHIPS
CHEEZIO

YEAH, IT WAS. HONESTLY? I ALMOST FORGOT WHAT HAVING FRIENDS WAS LIKE.
SOME OF THEM ARE REAL CHARACTERS...
YOUR ROUGHNECK BUDDIES HAVE GOT A LOT TO LEARN, HONEY.

HAH. I GUESS I DO TOO.
ETTA, BEFORE YOU LEAVE...CAN I SHOW YOU SOMETHING? IT WON'T TAKE LONG, AND--
--WELL, I KNOW IT'S LATE. YOU PROBABLY NEED TO GET HOME...

STEVE, IT'S THREE A.M. I'VE ALREADY MISSED MY BEDTIME.
OF COURSE YOU CAN, JUST QUIT BEIN' ALL NERVOUS ABOUT IT. YOU'RE MAKING MY ANXIETY FLARE UP.

THANKS. IT'S JUST A THING I'VE BEEN WORKING ON...I HAVEN'T SHOWN ANYONE YET.

SHOULD I COVER MY EYES? I DON'T NEED TO KNOW WHAT YOUR BROWSER HISTORY IS LOOKIN' LIKE THESE DAYS.
ETTA, THIS IS SERIOUS.

I'M NOT MUCH OF A FILMMAKER, BUT I'VE PUT A LOT OF TIME INTO THIS. I'M NOT SURE WHY. MAYBE IT'S HEALING IN SOME WAY?

I'M HONORED THAT YOU TRUST ME, STEVE.
WHATEVER IT IS, I'M SURE IT'S *GREAT.*

IT ISN'T DONE YET. I MEAN, I DON'T KNOW IF I'LL EVER EVEN *FINISH* IT--
YOU'RE REALLY BUILDING THIS UP, STEVE TREVOR. YOU PLAN ON LEAVING ME IN SUSPENSE ALL NIGHT?

IT'S A DOCUMENTARY...

...ABOUT *HER.*

IMMORTAL WONDER WOMAN
DO YOU THINK YOU COULD LIFT A TRUCK?
I KNOW I CAN LIFT A TRUCK...
WHAT IF IT WAS A TRUCK THAT, LIKE, HAD A TRAILER WITH OTHER TRUCKS ON IT?
HAH! YEAH, I BELIEVE SO.
WOULD IT BE HARD?
I DON'T THINK IT WOULD BE EASY!
WHAT CAN'T YOU LIFT?
PLENTY OF THINGS.
LIKE WHAT? NAME THEM.
OH, I DON'T KNOW!
I'LL TELL YOU IF I EVER FIND OUT.
THIS WAS WONDER WOMAN.
SHE WAS MY PERSONAL HERO...
...AND THE FIRST WOMAN I EVER LOVED.

--I HAVE COMPLETE FAITH THAT S.T.A.R. LABS WILL NOT ONLY TREAT HER WITH DIGNITY, BUT PROTECT THE PUBLIC FROM ANY FURTHER DISTURBANCES.
NOW IF YOU'LL EXCUSE ME--
--DID YOU GET THAT, JOHNNY?!
WHAT CAN YOU TELL US ABOUT THE MAXWELL LORD SITUATION?
HE WILL BE DEALT WITH.
CRISIS NARROWLY AVOIDED
52 NEWS
<--THIS APPEARS TO BE THE LAST OF THOSE TRAPPED IN THE FIRE...WE MAY HAVE MANAGED TO AVOID ANY CASUALTIES!>*
*TRANSLATED FROM FRENCH --BRITTANY
<THANKS TO HER, WONDER WOMAN! HAVE YOU ANYTHING TO SAY?>
OBTENIR DE L'AIDE.
HEROISM WEARS MANY HATS. WONDER WOMAN KNEW MORE THAN MOST THAT BEING A HERO OFTEN INVOLVES VIOLENT EXCHANGES, SNAP JUDGMENTS, AND MORAL GRAY AREAS.
HER FAVORITE VICTORIES WERE THE ONES THAT DIDN'T CALL FOR VIOLENCE.
SHE WAS AT HER HAPPIEST WHEN SHE WAS SIMPLY HELPING THOSE IN NEED.

--AND IT'S CLEAR THAT IF THE AIRPLANE CONTINUES TO LOSE ALTITUDE, THE OUTCOME COULD BE CATASTROPHIC--
METRO-NEWS 23
LIVE: EMERGENCY ON FLIGHT 824
--WAIT! SOMETHING HAS HAPPENED! THE PLANE APPEARS TO HAVE REGAINED SOME MEASURE OF CONTROL--
IT'S A MIRACLE!
WE'RE GETTING REPORTS FROM AIR TRAFFIC CONTROL THAT SOMETHING HAS CORRECTED THE FLIGHT PATH.
SHE WAS THE MIRACLE. SHE WAS ALWAYS THE MIRACLE.
WONDER WOMAN.
SHE DIDN'T EVEN STICK AROUND TO GET CREDIT.
THAT DAY SHE CAME HOME SMELLING LIKE JET FUEL, AND ASKED IF I FELT LIKE TAKE-OUT FOR DINNER.

NO ONE EVEN KNEW IT HAD BEEN HER--NOT UNTIL THE CELL PHONE FOOTAGE STARTED SHOWING UP.
THERE WERE A TOTAL OF 247 SOULS ABOARD THAT PLANE.
247 MORE PEOPLE WHO OWED THEIR LIVES TO HER.
BUT THIS WASN'T UNIQUE. THIS WASN'T A REMARKABLE MOMENT FOR HER.
TO WONDER WOMAN, IT WAS JUST AN AVERAGE DAY.
MODERN TIME
THE RESCUE OF FLIGHT 824
THIS WAS WHAT SHE DID.
HER HEROISM WAS SO HARD TO FATHOM THAT TO SOME IT BECAME A *MYTH.*
HER ACTIONS WERE SO GREAT AND UNIMAGINABLE, MANY SIMPLY COULDN'T BELIEVE IT.
TO HER, THIS WAS OF LITTLE CONCERN.

BUT IF YOU'RE GOING TO BE A HERO, YOU HAVE TO CONTEND WITH THOSE WHO HAVE TAKEN THE *OTHER* PATH.
SHE WOULDN'T LIKE ME USING THE WORD *VILLAINS,* BUT THAT'S WHAT I'D CALL THEM IF SHE WRAPPED ME IN HER LASSO.
SOME OF THEM HAD A TWISTED LOGIC BEHIND THEIR ACTIONS--
--WHILE OTHERS JUST SEEMED TO *HATE* HER.
SHE OFTEN WONDERED *WHY?* WHAT CAUSED CERTAIN PEOPLE TO LASH OUT THE WAY THEY DID?
IT'S A BIT OF A TIRED EXPRESSION, BUT I'VE ALWAYS THOUGHT IT WAS *TRUE,* WHAT THEY SAY ABOUT THE LIGHT AND THE DARK.
ONE CAN'T EXIST WITHOUT THE OTHER.
THROUGH THE YEARS SHE TRIED CHANGING IT UP, THINKING MAYBE A DIFFERENT APPROACH MIGHT HELP.
BUT EVEN WITH A NEW COSTUME...
...SHE WAS ALWAYS THE SAME WONDER WOMAN.
HEY. CAN YOU PAUSE THIS FOR A SEC?
SURE.

THIS IS WILD. WHERE DID YOU GET ALL THIS OLD FOOTAGE OF HER?
WELL, UH, SINCE SHE DIED I'VE SPENT A LOT OF TIME SEARCHING AROUND, TRYING TO ARCHIVE THIS STUFF. IT WASN'T ALL EASY TO FIND, BUT THERE'S A LOT OUT THERE.
THE DOCUMENTARY KIND OF CAME OUT OF THAT, I GUESS.
I JUST DON'T WANT TO--
I DON'T WANT THE WORLD TO FORGET HER.
THEY WON'T.
WE WON'T EITHER.
NOW KEEP IT GOING! THIS IS INCREDIBLE STUFF, STEVE.
ALWAYS POWERFUL, SHE WAS A FORCE OF NATURE--A FORCE FOR GOOD. SO MUCH SO THAT EVEN BELIEVERS STRUGGLED TO UNDERSTAND HOW SHE WORKED.
OH MY GOD, IS THAT...
THE INVISIBLE PLANE!
NO ONE WOULD EVER FULLY UNDERSTAND WHAT MADE HER TICK...
...MYSELF INCLUDED.

--SO YOU WERE SAYING THERE WAS A CLOSE CALL WITH THE PYROTECHNICS DURING FILMING?
UH, YEAH, IT SEEMS SOMEONE WAS ASLEEP AT THE WHEEL AND OVERLOADED THE CHARGES IN THE HELICOPTER SCENE.
IT WOULD HAVE BEEN REAL BAD, BUT WONDER WOMAN SHOWED UP AND SAVED THE DAY.
FRANKLY, SHE HAD BETTER TIMING THAN ANYONE ELSE ON SET!
MAXIMUM HOWL
SO, AS PART OF THE *JUSTICE LEAGUE* YOU'VE GOTTEN TO RUB SHOULDERS WITH SOME REAL HEROES!
I MEAN... I'M A HERO TOO--
--WHAT'S WONDER WOMAN LIKE? HOW TALL IS SHE?
SHE'S ABOUT MY HEIGHT.
REALLY? I ALWAYS THOUGHT SHE HAD A FEW INCHES ON YOU.
...MAYBE, LIKE ONE OR TWO. BUT--
CAN YOU TELL HER TO COME ON THE SHOW?
HA HA HA!
NOBODY KNEW HOW SHE DID IT, BUT THEY AGREED ALL THE SAME.
--WOULDN'T HAVE BEEN POSSIBLE WITHOUT WONDER WOMAN. SHE'S TRULY THE *BEST* OF US!
--I SUSPECT THIS WON'T BE THE *LAST* TIME I SAY IT, BUT WE ALL OWE OUR SURVIVAL TO WONDER WOMAN.
SHE WAS A SYMBOL FOR *PEACE*...
...BUT THAT'S NOT HOW *I* KNEW HER.

WAR.
PEOPLE TEND TO FORGET THAT WONDER WOMAN SPENT A LIFETIME IN PREPARATION FOR THE THING SHE HATED MOST.
AS SOLDIERS, WE HAVE TO BECOME NUMB.
WE COMMIT OURSELVES TO THE IDEA THAT WE'RE MAKING A DIFFERENCE, THAT WE'RE THE HEROES.
AT SOME POINTS, YOU KNOW YOU'RE SHAKING HANDS WITH THE DEVIL.
MAKING CONCESSIONS FOR THIS VAGUE IDEA OF THE GREATER GOOD.
BUT SHE REFUSED TO BE OKAY WITH COLLATERAL DAMAGE.
SHE WAS ON ONE SIDE, AND ONE SIDE ALONE.
TRUTH.

SOME OF US THINK WE KNOW WHO WE ARE. WE BECOME SO SURE OF IT, WE HANG ON TO IT LIKE A DIAMOND--
--A REFINED VERSION OF OUR IDENTITY.
WHEN TESTED, THOUGH, WE DISCOVER ITS FLAWS.
OUR BIASES, OUR BLIND SPOTS.
IT'S PAINFUL SEEING YOURSELF FOR THE FIRST TIME, BUT IT'S THROUGH THAT RECOGNITION THAT WE CAN BECOME BETTER.
SHE GAVE ME THAT.
HER EXAMPLE WAS A SHINING LIGHT THAT ALLOWED ME TO SEE.
LIKE AN ANGEL--MY ANGEL.
OH MY GOD, IS THAT--
YEAH. THAT'S ME.
SOMETIMES YOU GET SO LOST IN THE FOG OF WAR, YOU FORGET THAT PEACE IS EVEN AN OPTION.

WHEN I FIRST APPROACHED THE THEMYSCIRAN EMISSARY ABOUT FILMING THIS SPECIAL, SHE INITIALLY HAD NO INTEREST.
BUT AFTER WE PROMISED TO AIR THE SPEECH SHE GAVE AT THE U.N.'S *WORLD FREEDOM COUNCIL,* SHE AGREED TO SIT DOWN FOR AN EXCLUSIVE INTERVIEW.
WONDER WOMAN, YOU HAVE THE FLOOR.
THANK YOU FOR HAVING ME HERE TODAY. I PROMISE NOT TO TAKE UP TOO MUCH TIME.
AS AN AMBASSADOR TO MAN'S WORLD, I FIND MYSELF TROUBLED BY THE CLEARLY SELF-SERVING NATURE OF THIS PAST WEEK'S AGGRESSION.
I FIND IT *OFFENSIVE* TO SEE BLAME ASSIGNED TO THE VICTIMS IN THIS MATTER, AS I WAS PRESENT FOR THE SHELLING OF CIVILIAN HOMES--AN ACT THAT BREAKS THE R.O.E. OF ANY CIVILIZED NATION.
I REFUSE TO ACCEPT ANY EXCUSES OFFERED BY THE RESPONSIBLE PARTIES PRESENT HERE TODAY.
INSTEAD, I WOULD RATHER FOCUS ON THE TRUTH, AND THE *CONSEQUENCES* OF TRUTH.
I MAY BE A GUEST IN MAN'S WORLD, BUT I WILL NOT SIT IDLY BY AND WATCH YOU KILL FOR PROFIT.
I EXPECT THAT JUSTICE WILL BE DONE, AND THAT THOSE RESPONSIBLE WILL BE MADE TO *ANSWER* FOR THEIR CRIMES.
YOU CAN DO THIS NOW, OR I WILL SEE TO IT *MYSELF.*

THAT'S POWERFUL STUFF. THANK YOU FOR JOINING ME TODAY, WONDER WOMAN.
IT'S BEEN OVER A DECADE SINCE YOU GAVE THAT HISTORIC SPEECH AT THE U.N. SINCE THEN, HAVE YOU FELT LIKE YOUR WORDS HAVE MADE A CHANGE?
MAYBE, IN SOME SMALL WAYS. BEING A REPORTER, YOU KNOW AS WELL AS ANYONE THAT THERE IS ALWAYS MORE WORK TO BE DONE.
INDEED I DO. I REMEMBER EXACTLY WHERE I WAS WHEN I SAW YOUR SPEECH, TOO.
IT WAS VERY POIGNANT--HAVE YOU ALWAYS BEEN A GOOD PUBLIC SPEAKER?
THAT'S QUITE KIND OF YOU, MS. LANE, BUT I DON'T NEED TO SPEAK WELL.
I'M ARMED WITH SOMETHING MORE POWER-FUL THAN A COMMAND OF LANGUAGE COULD EVER OFFER.
THE *TRUTH* IS WHAT GIVES MY WORDS THEIR VALUE.
IF YOU WANT TO BE A GOOD SPEAKER, STOP THINKING ABOUT HOW WORDS WILL SERVE YOU. INSTEAD, FOCUS ON BEING OPEN TO WHAT THEIR AUTHENTICITY *TELLS* YOU.
BEAUTIFULLY SAID.

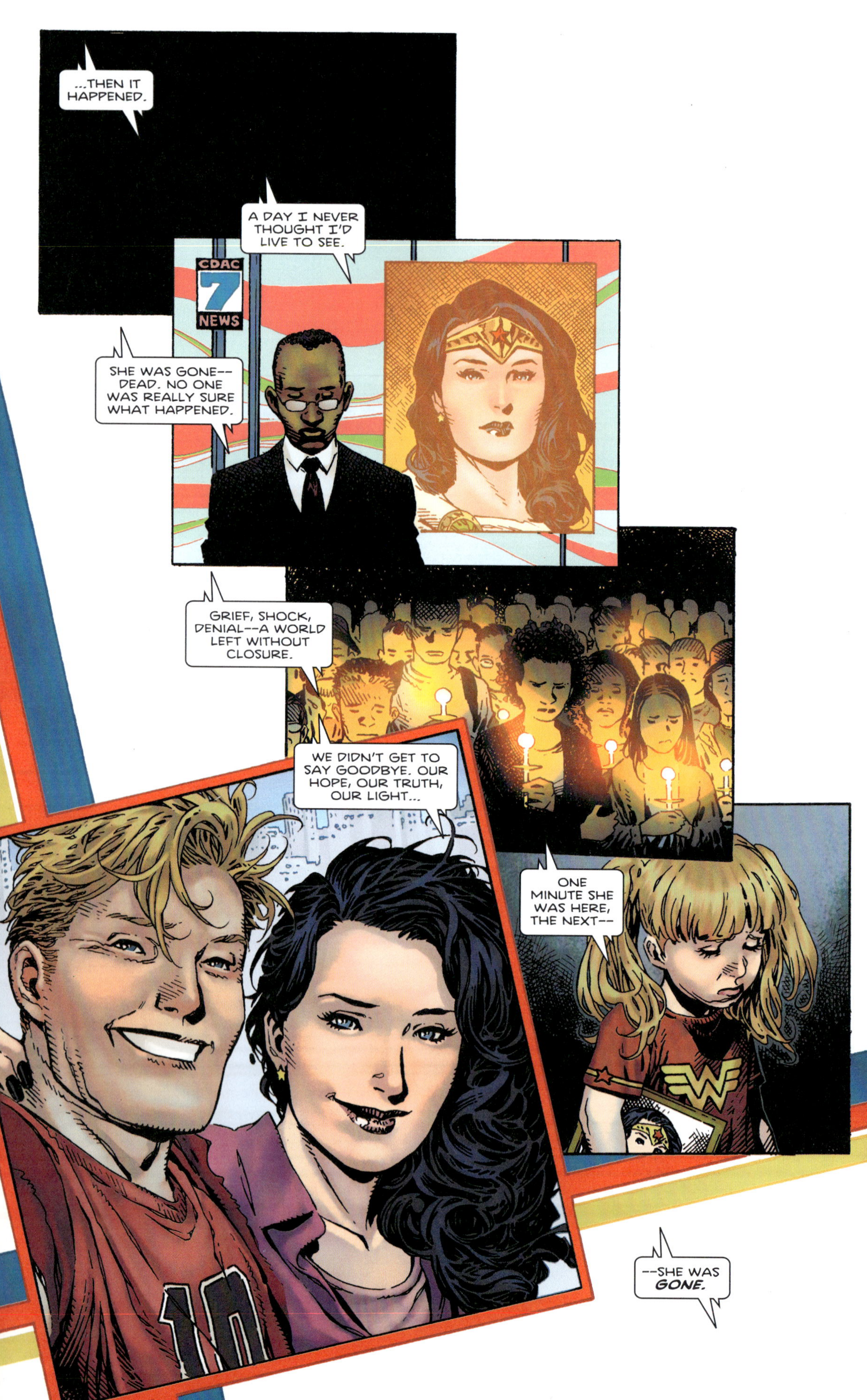

...THEN IT HAPPENED.
A DAY I NEVER THOUGHT I'D LIVE TO SEE.
CDAC 7 NEWS
SHE WAS GONE-- DEAD. NO ONE WAS REALLY SURE WHAT HAPPENED.
GRIEF, SHOCK, DENIAL--A WORLD LEFT WITHOUT CLOSURE.
WE DIDN'T GET TO SAY GOODBYE. OUR HOPE, OUR TRUTH, OUR LIGHT...
ONE MINUTE SHE WAS HERE, THE NEXT--
--SHE WAS *GONE.*

I...I DON'T KNOW HOW TO *END* IT.
IT FEELS TERRIBLE TO HAVE IT JUST...BE *THAT.* BUT FOR SOME REASON I CAN'T GET MYSELF TO FINISH IT EITHER.
IT'S LIKE... THEN SHE'LL *REALLY* BE GONE.

THAT'S DEATH THOUGH, ISN'T IT? I JUST HOPE WHEN MY STORY ENDS, SOMEONE MAKES A MOVIE ABOUT ME.
BUT SERIOUSLY, IT'S A BEAUTIFUL TRIBUTE. ARE YOU...
STEVE, ARE YOU ALL RIGHT?

YEAH. I GUESS, AS ALL RIGHT AS I CAN BE. THINGS ARE GOING GOOD WITH--
OH MY GOD!

YOU HAVEN'T *SHOWN* HER THIS, HAVE YOU?
NO, JEEZ! C'MON, ETTA--I KNOW I CAN BE A LITTLE DIM, BUT I'M NOT A *TOTAL* IDIOT.
GOOD. KEEP IT THAT WAY. I'M GLAD YOU'VE GOT SOMEONE SPECIAL, BUT *NO* GIRL NEEDS THE EXTRA PRESSURE OF LIVING UP TO *ALL THAT!*

ANYWAY, IT'S GOOD TO SEE YOU *SMILING* AGAIN. IT REALLY HAS BEEN A SPECIAL NIGHT.
BUT NOW IT'S SO LATE THAT IT'S EARLY! I'M GONNA HEAD OUT.
WANT ME TO CALL YOU A CAB?

THANKS, HON, BUT I GOT A CAR COMING!
GET HOME SAFE, ETTA. I'LL SEE YOU ON MONDAY. AND THANK YOU FOR...YOU KNOW.
EVERYTHING.
YOU GOT MY NUMBER IF YOU NEED ANYTHING. NOW GO GET SOME REST.

WE SPLIT NOT LONG BEFORE SHE DIED.
IT WASN'T LIKE WE HAD FALLEN OUT OF LOVE, NOTHING LIKE THAT...

...IT JUST FELT LIKE THE RIGHT THING TO DO. FOR BOTH OF US.
WE NEEDED SPACE...TO HEAL. TO GROW.

THE TWO OF US REALIZED WE WERE BEING STRONG FOR EACH OTHER.
WE NEEDED TO REMIND OURSELVES THAT WE COULD BE STRONG...
Steve

...ALONE.
IN MEMORIAM
MICHAEL W. CONRAD & BECKY CLOONAN WRITERS
JIM CHEUNG ARTIST MARCELO MAIOLO COLORIST
PAT BROSSEAU LETTERER BIXIE MATHIEU ASSISTANT EDITOR
BRITTANY HOLZHERR EDITOR MIKE COTTON SENIOR EDITOR

If you're still living in D.C. and I'm away, look to the east, in the direction of Themyscira. I will be there...thinking of you.
--Diana
5:47 AM
babe (3 missed calls)
News
Daily Planet
BREAKING: Multiple Wonder Woman sightings reported...

Wonder Woman #780 cover
by TRAVIS G. MOORE and
TAMRA BONVILLAIN

Wonder Woman #780
variant cover by
BECKY CLOONAN

HALL OF JUSTICE
CRINKLE
SZZZZCKT
DIANA?!

J'ONN...! THANK THE GODS, I FINALLY MADE IT *HOME!*
HOW UNEXPECTED.
THAT IS TO SAY, WELCOME BACK, DIANA.
...CARE FOR A COOKIE?
WHERE THE HEART IS
MICHAEL W. CONRAD & BECKY CLOONAN WRITERS TRAVIS MOORE (P. 1-22 & 30) & STEVE PUGH (P. 23-29) ARTISTS
TAMRA BONVILLAIN COLORIST PAT BROSSEAU LETTERER TRAVIS MOORE & TAMRA BONVILLAIN COVER
BECKY CLOONAN VARIANT COVER BIXIE MATHIEU ASSISTANT EDITOR BRITTANY HOLZHERR EDITOR MIKE COTTON SENIOR EDITOR
WONDER WOMAN CREATED BY WILLIAM MOULTON MARSTON
SUPERMAN CREATED BY JERRY SIEGEL AND JOE SHUSTER. BY SPECIAL ARRANGEMENT WITH THE JERRY SIEGEL FAMILY.

LATER...
DIANA? IT REALLY IS YOU!
YES! BACK FROM... WELL, MANY PLACES.
WHEN J'ONN TOLD ME, AT FIRST I THOUGHT HE WAS ATTEMPTING TO TELL A JOKE. I'VE NEVER BEEN MORE HAPPY TO BE WRONG.
I'M SO GLAD YOU'VE RETURNED!
I AM TOO, CLARK.
VERY LITTLE SURPRISES ME-- A FACT THAT I PRIDE MYSELF ON.
HELLO, BRUCE.
CONGRATULATIONS, DIANA... I WASN'T EXPECTING THIS.
THAT'S IT? A HANDSHAKE, THEN BACK TO BROODING?
WELL, I HAVE TO GET BACK TO GOTHAM, AND--
AND WHAT? DIANA IS BACK!
OF COURSE WE'LL CATCH YOU UP ON EVERYTHING THAT'S HAPPENED SINCE YOU WERE, YOU KNOW...AWAY. BUT FOR NOW...
...LET'S TAKE A MOMENT AND JUST FEEL THANKFUL.

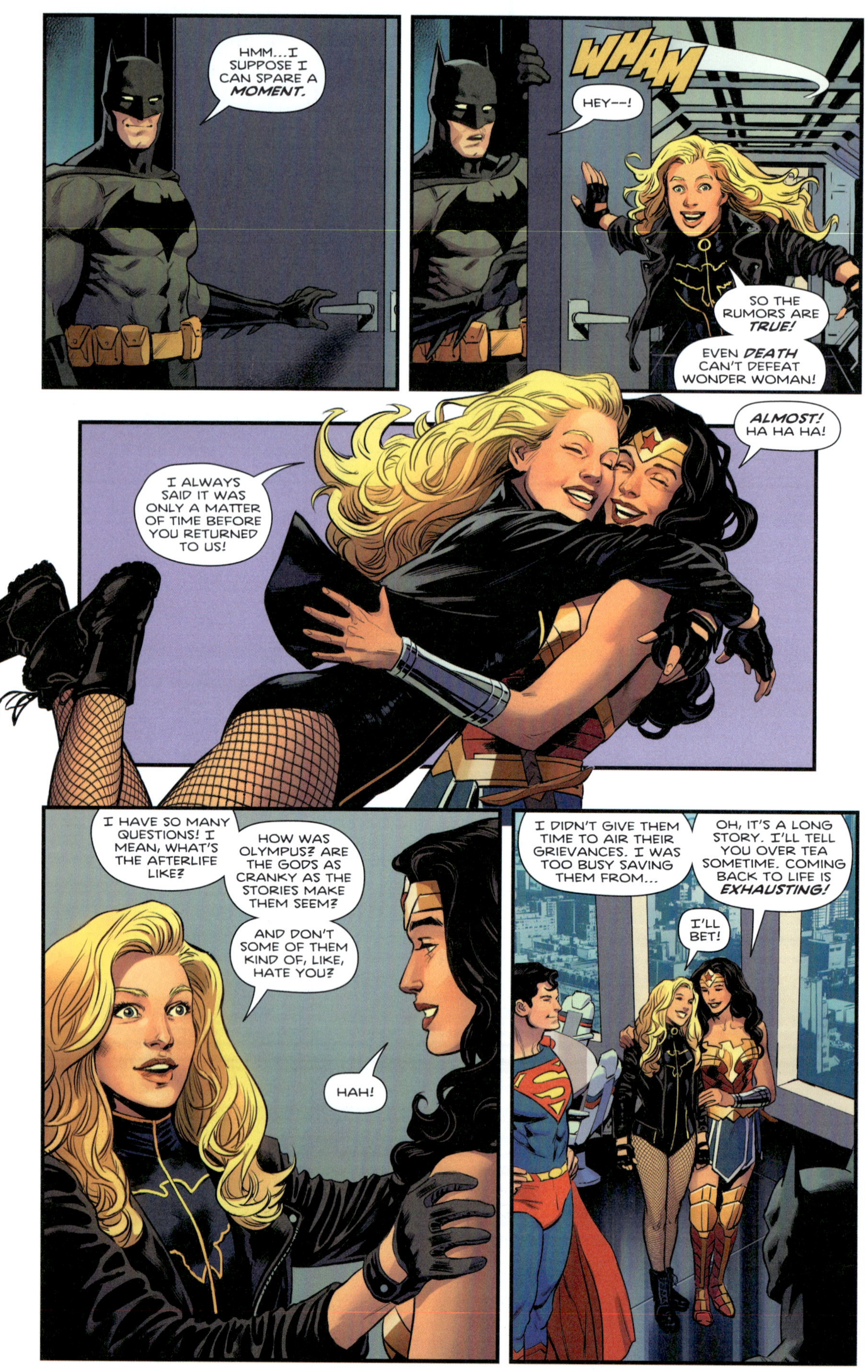
HMM...I SUPPOSE I CAN SPARE A MOMENT.
WHAM
HEY--!
SO THE RUMORS ARE TRUE!
EVEN DEATH CAN'T DEFEAT WONDER WOMAN!
I ALWAYS SAID IT WAS ONLY A MATTER OF TIME BEFORE YOU RETURNED TO US!
ALMOST! HA HA HA!
I HAVE SO MANY QUESTIONS! I MEAN, WHAT'S THE AFTERLIFE LIKE?
HOW WAS OLYMPUS? ARE THE GODS AS CRANKY AS THE STORIES MAKE THEM SEEM?
AND DON'T SOME OF THEM KIND OF, LIKE, HATE YOU?
HAH!
I DIDN'T GIVE THEM TIME TO AIR THEIR GRIEVANCES. I WAS TOO BUSY SAVING THEM FROM...
OH, IT'S A LONG STORY. I'LL TELL YOU OVER TEA SOMETIME. COMING BACK TO LIFE IS EXHAUSTING!
I'LL BET!

IT DIDN'T TAKE LONG FOR DIANA TO FEEL AT HOME AGAIN, SURROUNDED BY FRIENDS AND LOVED ONES.
THEY ASKED HER WHERE SHE'D BEEN, WHAT SHE'D DONE, HOW SHE MANAGED TO RETURN. THEY WANTED TO KNOW EVERYTHING--
--BUT DIANA ALSO HAD QUESTIONS OF HER OWN.
SO MUCH HAD CHANGED IN HER ABSENCE...
...BUT SHE COULD WORRY ABOUT ALL THAT LATER.
RIGHT THEN, SHE WAS CONTENT TO SHARE STORIES, LAUGHS, AND HUGS.
OF COURSE, SHE KEPT A FEW DETAILS TO HERSELF.
A GIRL'S GOTTA HAVE SOME SECRETS.

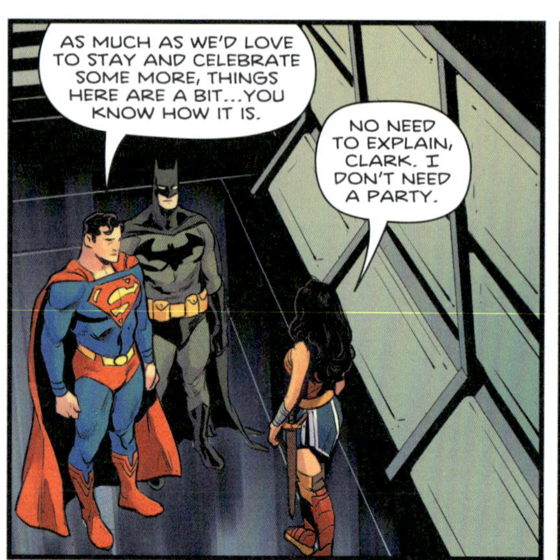
AS MUCH AS WE'D LOVE TO STAY AND CELEBRATE SOME MORE, THINGS HERE ARE A BIT...YOU KNOW HOW IT IS.
NO NEED TO EXPLAIN, CLARK. I DON'T NEED A PARTY.

IN FACT, GETTING BACK TO WORK SOUNDS LIKE JUST WHAT THE DOCTOR ORDERED...
DIANA!

I CAME AS SOON AS I HEARD!
EXCUSE THE INTERRUPTION-- THE JUSTICE LEAGUE DARK NEEDS YOUR HELP AT ONCE.*
SOUNDS LIKE DOCTOR FATE HAD THE SAME IDEA. GO, DIANA. WE'LL CATCH UP LATER.
*SEE JUSTICE LEAGUE #68 FOR MORE DETAILS! -- BRITTANY

GOOD TO HAVE YOU HOME, DIANA.
I'LL SEE YOU BOTH AGAIN SOON.
SO WHAT'S THE PROBLEM?
I'LL EXPLAIN ON THE WAY. COME, THERE'S NO TIME TO LOSE.

IT'S ATLANTIS...
SOMETHING IS TERRIBLY WRONG, AND WE NEED YOU--
HALT!
TAKE NOT ANOTHER STEP.

Diana will not be swept up into one of your **bizarre affairs**--not before having a moment of respite.
Can't you see she's clearly tired? She needs **rest!**
DOCTOR FATE, I'LL CONNECT WITH YOU SHORTLY. I NEED TO EXPLAIN TO MY DOTING MOTHER THAT I'VE BEEN **RESTING IN PEACE** FOR **FAR** TOO LONG ALREADY.
Doting?! Why, I merely--
MOTHER...
...I MISSED YOU.
--Oh!
My daughter...I never doubted that I would see you again. Not even in my darkest hour.

SO THE OLYMPIANS HAD ENOUGH SENSE TO KNOW THAT YOU SERVE A GREATER PURPOSE HERE AMONG US, WAS THAT IT?

NOT EXACTLY, NO. THE OLYMPIANS REMAIN AS UNCONCERNED ABOUT THIS WORLD AS EVER.

WOULD IT SURPRISE YOU TO HEAR THAT I ***FOUGHT*** MY WAY BACK?

HAH! OF ***COURSE*** YOU DID. I'M MERELY SAYING...

...YOU SAVED US.

YOU SAVED THE ***MULTIVERSE.***

YES, MOTHER, I MAY HAVE DONE THESE THINGS.

BUT I HEAR YOU'VE HAD YOUR HANDS FULL TOO, HERE IN MAN'S WORLD.

WHICH I'M SURE HASN'T BEEN IDEAL FOR YOU, AND FOR THAT I AM SORRY.

YOU WOULD APOLOGIZE FOR SACRIFICING YOURSELF!

PYTHIA PRESERVE ME, I HAVE RAISED A MASOCHIST.

DIANA, YOU HAVE NOTHING TO ATONE FOR. YOU'VE GIVEN ALL. YOU ARE THE ***HERO*** YOU WERE BORN TO BE.

HERO?
SAVE THE HONORIFICS FOR THOSE WHO REQUIRE SUCH A TITLE TO SUSTAIN THEIR EFFORTS.
I'M A WOMAN WHO CAN, AND SO I ***SHALL.***

HA HA HA! SO RARELY DO WE SEE WHO WE ***TRULY*** ARE.
THOUGH PART OF ME SUSPECTS YOU'RE MORE AWARE OF YOUR DEEDS THAN YOU CARE TO ADMIT.
IT MATTERS NOT.
YOU ASCENDED TO YOUR RIGHTFUL PLACE ON OLYMPUS, YET YOU REFUSED DIVINITY...
I CAN'T SAY I UNDERSTAND YOUR CHOICE TO RETURN, BUT I ***RESPECT*** IT.

YOU WISH THAT I HAD STAYED?

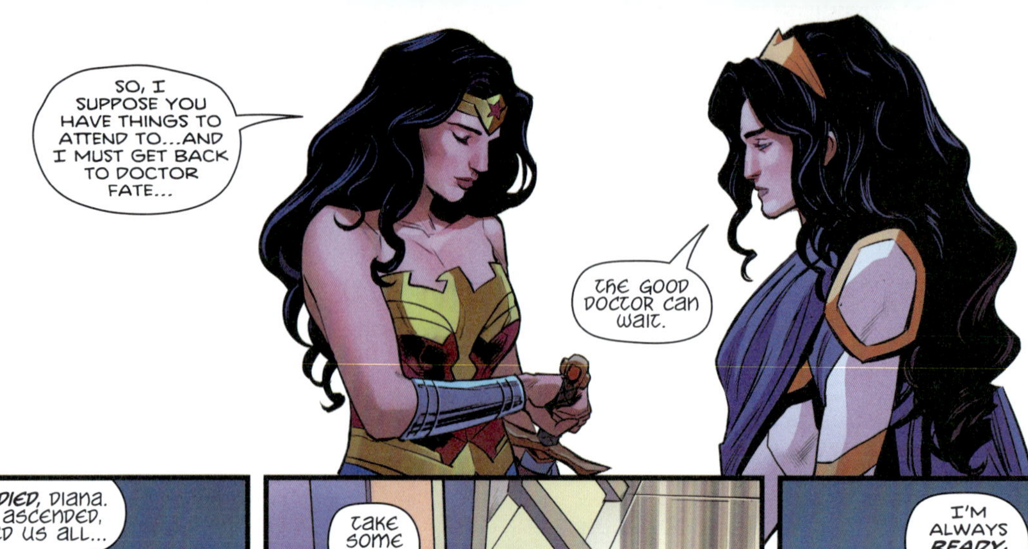
SO, I SUPPOSE YOU HAVE THINGS TO ATTEND TO...AND I MUST GET BACK TO DOCTOR FATE...
THE GOOD DOCTOR CAN WAIT.

YOU *DIED*, DIANA. YOU ASCENDED, SAVED US ALL...

TAKE SOME TIME.
RETURN TO THEMYSCIRA, AND DON'T LET THE LEAGUE PULL YOU IN ON ANY OF THEIR MISSIONS UNTIL YOU'RE READY.

I'M ALWAYS *READY,* MOTHER.

IN DEATH, I SAW MANY THINGS. I *CHOSE* TO COME BACK, AND I ALONE WILL DECIDE WHAT MY NEXT STEP WILL BE.
I KNOW WHAT AWAITS ME BEYOND THE VEIL, ALMOST MORE THAN I KNOW WHAT TOMORROW WILL BRING.
I...I FIND LITTLE COMFORT IN THIS.

REST, IF ONLY FOR A DAY.

DIANA RELENTED. SHE DECIDED TO RETURN TO THE ISLAND, THEMYSCIRA.
IT WAS A CHOICE THAT REQUIRED LITTLE CONSIDERATION, AND SEEMED THE MOST APPROPRIATE, AND SIMPLE, RESPONSE.
HOWEVER, TURNING OFF WAS NEVER SOMETHING THAT CAME NATURALLY TO HER.
SHE WAS TIRED, YES. WHO WOULDN'T BE? BUT SHE COULDN'T STOP HER MIND FROM RACING.
COGITO ERGO SUM. I THINK, THEREFORE I AM.
BUT SHE FELT MOST ALIVE, MOST REAL, WHEN SHE WASN'T THINKING.
SHE NEEDED TO BE RESPONDING, ACTING, ACCOMPLISHING.
BEING THE THING SHE CLAIMED NOT TO BE...
<H-HELP!>*
COUGH
<PLEASE!>
KREAAAKK
SPLOOSH
*TRANSLATED FROM TURKISH. -- BRITTANY.

...A HERO.
SKLASH
TAKE HER! I'LL GET THE OTHERS!
BE STILL. I'VE GOT YOU.
SPLOOSH
<MY GOD, WHAT IS HAPPENING?>
KREAAAK
<SHE'S LIFTING US!>

KRREE-WOUGH
HUNGH!
WHOOSH
<LOOK OUT! A FLYING BOAT!>
<IS THAT A WOMAN UNDER IT?>
<WAIT! THAT'S-->

IT'S WONDER WOMAN!

THIS MAN NEEDS FIRST AID!
BE CAREFUL WITH THEM. THEY NEED WATER.
RIGHT AWAY!
<BRING THE WATER, AND BLANKETS TOO!>

WONDER WOMAN! OVER HERE!
WE THOUGHT YOU WERE DEAD!

WELL, YES. I WAS.
BUT AS YOU CAN SEE, I'M BACK--NOW PUT THAT THING DOWN AND HELP.

YOU SAVED US. THANK YOU.
I ONLY DID WHAT I COULD.
NOW WAIT HERE, I'LL FIND SOMEONE TO WRAP YOUR ARM.

<DID YOU SEE THAT? YOU ALL SAW THAT, RIGHT?>
<THAT WAS WONDER WOMAN! I CAN'T BELIEVE IT!>

<I GOT THE WHOLE THING ON VIDEO!>
<EXTRAORDINARY! I NEVER THOUGHT I'D SEE SOMETHING SO...>

THE BETTER PART OF A YEAR HAD PASSED SINCE THE LAST TIME DIANA HAD FLOWN HOME. SHE HAD BEEN AWAY FOR TOO LONG, AND THE WORLD HAD KEPT TURNING WITHOUT HER.
IN A WAY, THE THOUGHT WAS REASSURING.
WHEN SHE DIED, SHE HAD TO LEAVE EVERYONE SHE CARED ABOUT BEHIND. SHE'D BEEN PREPARED TO GIVE IT ALL UP--**FOREVER,** IF NEED BE.
BUT SHE WAS BACK NOW.
IT WASN'T HER BEATING HEART, THE SUN ON HER SKIN, OR THE WIND ON HER FACE...
...IT WAS BEING ABLE TO MAKE A DIFFERENCE.
THAT WAS HOW SHE KNEW SHE WAS ALIVE.

GREENWAY APARTMENTS, WASHINGTON, D.C.
BILLS, JUNK, BILLS... C'MON.

WHAT THE--?!

Planet
WONDER WOMAN IS BACK!
Multiple Sightings Across the Atlantic
TOK

DAILY PLANET
Multiple Sightings Across the Atlantic

YES!

GATEWAY CITY MEGAMALL.
BAT BURGER
WAIT A MINUTE. DOES THAT SAY...
SSSH!
BREAKING NEWS WONDER WOMAN RETURNS
BREAKING NEWS WONDER WOMAN RETURNS
BREAKING NEWS WON
--REPORTS HAVE BEEN POURING IN EARLY THIS MORNING OF WONDER WOMAN SEEN LIFTING A CAPSIZED BOAT CARRYING REFUGEES--
DONNA, ARE YOU SEEING THIS?!
IT CAN'T BE--
--SHE CAME BACK?!
CASSIE, SHE'S BACK!
THIS TAKES PLACE AFTER THE EVENTS OF WONDER GIRL #4. -- BRITTANY
YEAH!
SHE CAME BACK!
IT'S A MIRACLE!
CLAP CLAP CLAP

OLLIDAY CLUBHOUSE.
--SIGHTINGS HAVE BEEN CONFIRMED BY WHAT APPEARS TO BE VIDEO FOOTAGE CAPTURED BY RESCUE WORKERS STATIONED ON A SMALL ISLAND OUTSIDE OF--
SHE'S BACK, Y'ALL!
I TOLD YA! NOTHING CAN KEEP OUR GIRL DOWN!
HOLLIDAY GIRLS
SEND UP THE SIGNAL! AND TELL THE OTHERS TO TAKE THE DAY OFF--
IT'S A *HOLIDAY!*
BRRRAAAH
DOWNTOWN WASHINGTON, D.C.
NEWS WONDER WOMAN RETURNS-MULTIPLE
OH--!

QURAC, BANA-MIGHDALL STRONGHOLD.
OOOO-RAHHH!
KRAK-KRAKA-KRAK
WHAT'S ALL THIS RACKET?! AND WHY DO YOU ABANDON YOUR POSTS?
KRAK-KRAKA-KRAK
LADY ARTEMIS, YOU HAVEN'T HEARD?!
DIANA IS BACK!
OUR CHAMPION HAS RISEN!
KRAK-KRAK-KRAK
YES-- AND? WE ARE WARRIORS. SAVE THE REVERIE AND RETURN TO YOUR DUTIES.
AND FIND QUEEN FARUKA. I MUST SPEAK TO HER AT ONCE.
THEMYSCIRA.
IF WHAT YOU SAY IS INDEED TRUE...
...THEN IT IS INCREDIBLE. YET SOMEHOW, I KNEW IT EVEN BEFORE YOU TOLD ME. I WILL INFORM THE OTHERS IMMEDIATELY.
SISTERS! A MOMENT OF YOUR TIME...
MANY OF US HAVE FELT A STIRRING DEEP WITHIN OUR SOULS--A SENSE THAT SOMETHING IMPOSSIBLE, SOMETHING WE SCARCELY DARED HOPE FOR, WAS UPON US.
OUR INSTINCTS WERE CORRECT. THE DAY HAS COME!
DIANA HAS RETURNED!

BAR PIRATA, SÃO PAULO.

<--SEEMINGLY RISEN FROM THE DEAD, WONDER WOMAN HAS MADE A MIRACULOUS RETURN TO EARTH-->*

SAÚDE!

YEAAH!

HA HA HA!

TCHIM-TCHIM

*TRANSLATED FROM PORTUGUESE. -- BRITTANY

<HEY, WATCH IT!>

PARTS UNKNOWN.

SHE DID IT...SHE ACTUALLY DID IT.

Wonder Woman Returns

...INCONCEIVABLE!

BRIIINGBRIING

H--HELLO?

YES, OF COURSE I'VE SEEN--

YES. I AGREE. WE HAVE TO GET AHEAD OF THIS.

I'LL BE THERE RIGHT AWAY.

LATER...

SHE'S HERE!

HURRAH! HURRAH!

DIANA!

SHE HAS RETURNED!

WE SHOULD HAVE KNOWN. EVEN DEATH CANNOT STOP YOU.

WHEN I FIRST ARRIVED, I WASN'T SURE WHAT KIND OF WORLD I WOULD BE RETURNING TO.

IT IS A GREAT COMFORT KNOWING OUR ISLAND AND HER PEOPLE ARE IN GOOD HANDS, ***QUEEN NUBIA.***

YES, WELL...WITH HIPPOLYTA IN MAN'S WORLD, ***SOMEONE*** HAD TO MAINTAIN ORDER HERE.

IT HASN'T BEEN EASY. TENSIONS HAVE BEEN HIGH.*

*SEE NUBIA & THE AMAZONS! -- BRITTANY.

EACH ONE OF THEM HAD MISSED DIANA FOR HER OWN REASONS...
LONG LIVE DIANA!
...BUT THEY ALL SHARED IN THE SAME EUPHORIC RELIEF OF HAVING HER BACK WHERE SHE WAS MOST LOVED.
TO-TOOOM
TO-TOOOM
EVERYONE HAD STORIES TO SHARE, MEMORIES BOTH GOOD AND BAD.
THEY EACH WANTED TO TELL HER WHAT THEY HADN'T BEEN ABLE TO, BACK BEFORE IT HAD ALL HAPPENED.
IT WAS A TRIUMPHANT NIGHT. JOYOUS...AND OVERWHELMING.

THE JOURNEY HOME HAD BEEN A LONG ONE.
SLIPPING AWAY FROM YOUR OWN HOMECOMING PARTY, I SEE?
IT'S A LOT. I APOLOGIZE, MY QUEEN. I JUST HAVEN'T HAD A MOMENT TO MYSELF. NOT SINCE...
BELIEVE ME, I UNDERSTAND, AND I'M NOT ABOUT TO STOP YOU. I ONLY WANT A MOMENT BEFORE YOU RETIRE FOR THE EVENING.
AND WITHOUT THE FORMALITIES. I WOULD HAVE US TALK AS WE USED TO.*
*SEE WONDER WOMAN 80TH ANNIVERSARY 100-PAGE SUPER SPECTACULAR #1 -- BRITTANY.
OF COURSE, NUBIA.

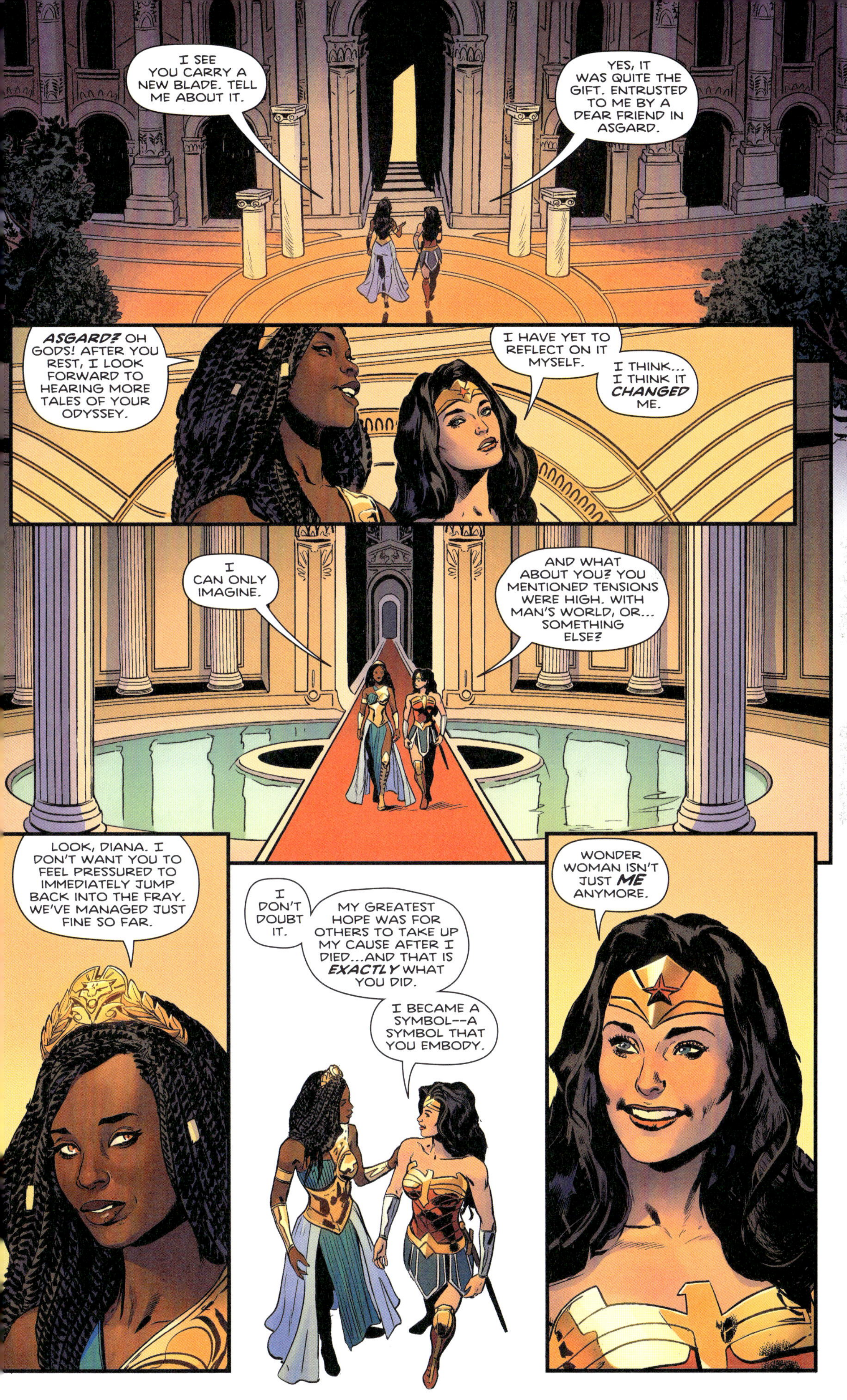
I SEE YOU CARRY A NEW BLADE. TELL ME ABOUT IT.
YES, IT WAS QUITE THE GIFT. ENTRUSTED TO ME BY A DEAR FRIEND IN ASGARD.
ASGARD? OH GODS! AFTER YOU REST, I LOOK FORWARD TO HEARING MORE TALES OF YOUR ODYSSEY.
I HAVE YET TO REFLECT ON IT MYSELF.
I THINK... I THINK IT CHANGED ME.
I CAN ONLY IMAGINE.
AND WHAT ABOUT YOU? YOU MENTIONED TENSIONS WERE HIGH. WITH MAN'S WORLD, OR... SOMETHING ELSE?
LOOK, DIANA. I DON'T WANT YOU TO FEEL PRESSURED TO IMMEDIATELY JUMP BACK INTO THE FRAY. WE'VE MANAGED JUST FINE SO FAR.
I DON'T DOUBT IT.
MY GREATEST HOPE WAS FOR OTHERS TO TAKE UP MY CAUSE AFTER I DIED...AND THAT IS EXACTLY WHAT YOU DID.
I BECAME A SYMBOL--A SYMBOL THAT YOU EMBODY.
WONDER WOMAN ISN'T JUST ME ANYMORE.

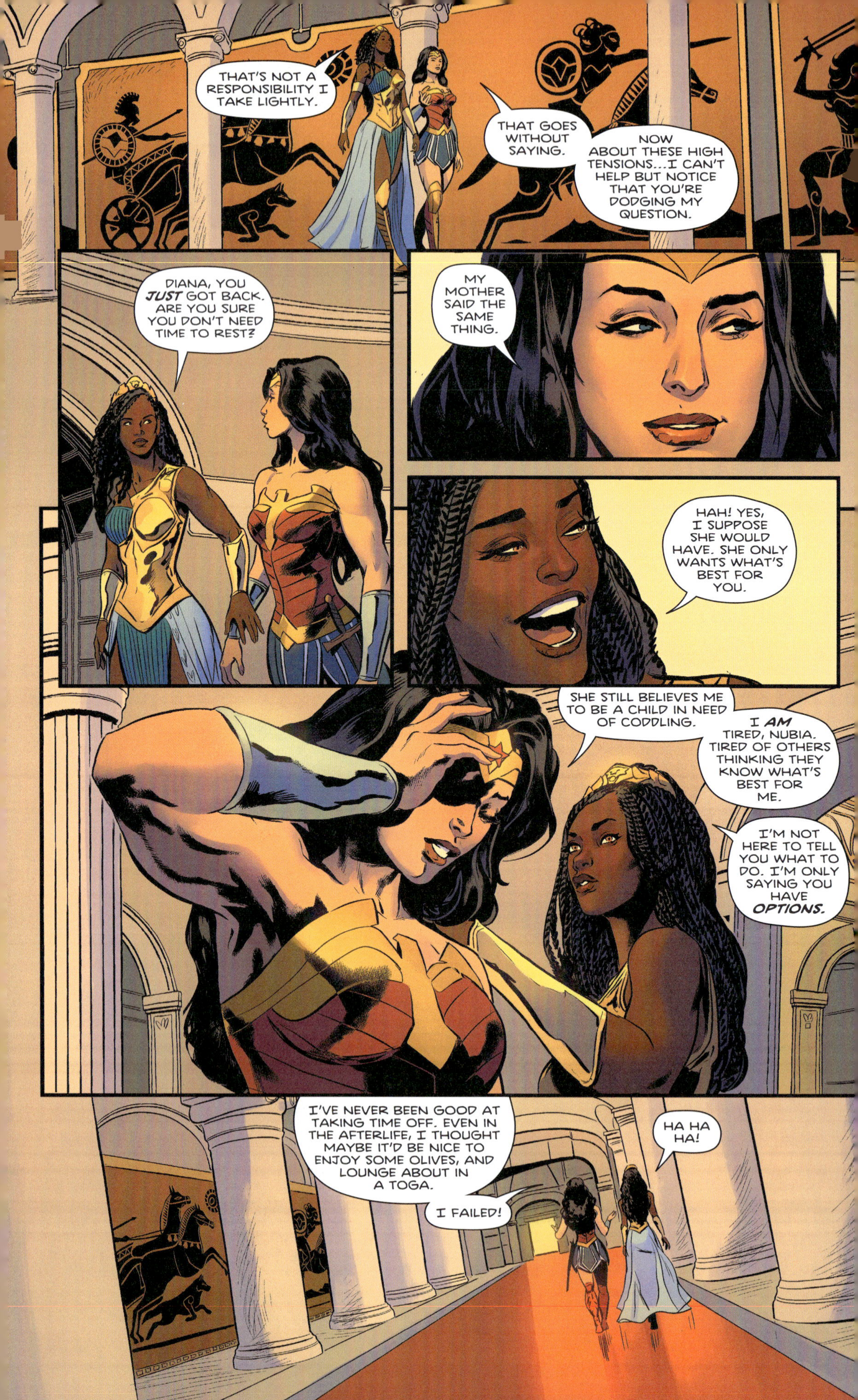
THAT'S NOT A RESPONSIBILITY I TAKE LIGHTLY.
THAT GOES WITHOUT SAYING.
NOW ABOUT THESE HIGH TENSIONS...I CAN'T HELP BUT NOTICE THAT YOU'RE DODGING MY QUESTION.
DIANA, YOU JUST GOT BACK. ARE YOU SURE YOU DON'T NEED TIME TO REST?
MY MOTHER SAID THE SAME THING.
HAH! YES, I SUPPOSE SHE WOULD HAVE. SHE ONLY WANTS WHAT'S BEST FOR YOU.
SHE STILL BELIEVES ME TO BE A CHILD IN NEED OF CODDLING.
I AM TIRED, NUBIA. TIRED OF OTHERS THINKING THEY KNOW WHAT'S BEST FOR ME.
I'M NOT HERE TO TELL YOU WHAT TO DO. I'M ONLY SAYING YOU HAVE OPTIONS.
I'VE NEVER BEEN GOOD AT TAKING TIME OFF. EVEN IN THE AFTERLIFE, I THOUGHT MAYBE IT'D BE NICE TO ENJOY SOME OLIVES, AND LOUNGE ABOUT IN A TOGA.
I FAILED!
HA HA HA!

AH, HERE WE ARE.
I AM SIMPLY DOING AS I WAS TOLD.
MOTHER WILL SEND ME BACK TO OLYMPUS IF SHE HEARS WE ENTERED HER PRIVATE CHAMBERS WITHOUT HER PERMISSION.
BEFORE SHE LEFT, HIPPOLYTA GAVE ME *THIS.*
SHE TOLD ME, "WHEN DIANA RETURNS, MAKE CERTAIN SHE IS GIVEN WHAT IS HERS."
WHAT IS MINE...?
SHE NEVER GAVE UP HOPE. IT WAS ALMOST LIKE SHE *KNEW...*
SHE EVEN FORBADE THEIR USE.
I DON'T THINK SHE WANTED ANY OF US TO GET *TOO* COMFORTABLE WITH THE IDEA THAT YOU WERE GONE.
IT SEEMS AS IF SHE WAS COUNTING ON YOUR RETURN...I SUSPECT SHE KNEW THE *TRUTH* ALL ALONG...
...THAT ONE DAY YOU'D FIND YOUR WAY BACK TO US.

THANK YOU, NUBIA.
SISTER, JOIN ME IN THIS RENEWAL OF VOWS.
THAT HESTIA MAY KNOW WE STILL HONOR THE VIRTUES.
I PLEDGE MY LIFE TO TRUTH. THIS IS MY COVENANT.
I PLEDGE MY LIFE TO UNDER-STANDING. THIS IS MY COVENANT.

I TRUST YOU WILL SLEEP EASY TONIGHT, BACK IN YOUR OWN BED. WE WILL SPEAK MORE TOMORROW.
MY OWN BED! IT SOUNDS LIKE A DREAM ALREADY. GIVE MY BEST TO ANY WARRIORS WHO STILL ENJOY THE FESTIVITIES.
I SUSPECT THEIR CELEBRATION WILL STILL BE IN FULL SWING WHEN YOU WAKE.
AMAZONS DO KNOW HOW TO PARTY.
SIGH
IT WAS A LOT TO TAKE IN.
MAYBE IT HAD BEEN THE TRAUMA OF DYING...OR PERHAPS IT WAS THE ORDEAL OF REBIRTH...
...WHATEVER THE CASE, THERE WAS NO DOUBT THAT SOMETHING ABOUT HER WAS DIFFERENT...
...BUT SHE COULD THINK ABOUT THAT TOMORROW.

DIANA WOKE THE FOLLOWING MORNING WITH A CLEAR MIND AND A FULL HEART.
MUCH LIKE HER, THE WORLD HAD CHANGED. THE DIFFERENCES WERE SUBTLE, PERHAPS, BUT SHE FELT THEM ACUTELY.
THE FACT THAT SHE STILL HAD A PLACE IN IT WAS NEVER IN QUESTION...
...BUT WHAT EXACTLY HER NEW ROLE WAS GOING TO BE?
SHE WOULD ENJOY FIGURING THAT OUT.

Wonder Woman 2021 Annual #1
cover by MITCH GERADS

Wonder Woman 2021 Annual #1
variant cover by CARLOS D'ANDA

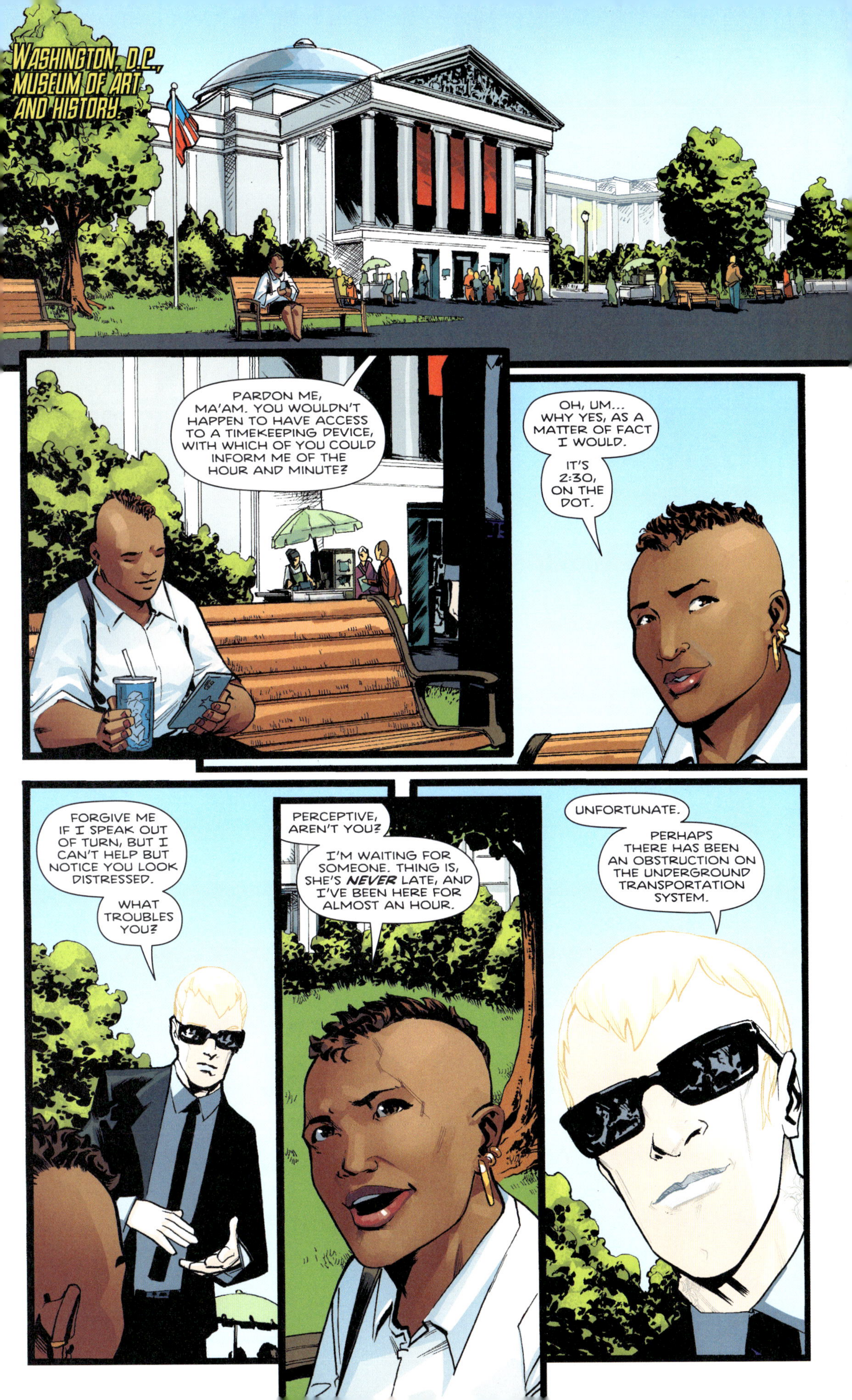

WASHINGTON, D.C., MUSEUM OF ART AND HISTORY
PARDON ME, MA'AM. YOU WOULDN'T HAPPEN TO HAVE ACCESS TO A TIMEKEEPING DEVICE, WITH WHICH OF YOU COULD INFORM ME OF THE HOUR AND MINUTE?
OH, UM... WHY YES, AS A MATTER OF FACT I WOULD.
IT'S 2:30, ON THE DOT.
FORGIVE ME IF I SPEAK OUT OF TURN, BUT I CAN'T HELP BUT NOTICE YOU LOOK DISTRESSED.
WHAT TROUBLES YOU?
PERCEPTIVE, AREN'T YOU?
I'M WAITING FOR SOMEONE. THING IS, SHE'S *NEVER* LATE, AND I'VE BEEN HERE FOR ALMOST AN HOUR.
UNFORTUNATE.
PERHAPS THERE HAS BEEN AN OBSTRUCTION ON THE UNDERGROUND TRANSPORTATION SYSTEM.

YEAH, THE SUBWAY IS PROBABLY JUST LATE.
IF WE'RE GONNA CHAT, MIGHT AS WELL HAVE A SEAT. I'M GONNA STRAIN MY NECK TALKIN' TO YOU LIKE THIS.
APOLOGIES, MY MANNERS ARE A WORK IN PROGRESS.
I'M NOT FROM AROUND HERE, YOU SEE.
YOU DON'T SAY? I NEVER WOULDA GUESSED!
HAH!
IS IT THAT OBVIOUS?
HARDLY ANYONE IN THIS CITY IS ACTUALLY *FROM* HERE.
SO WHAT DO THEY CALL YOU BACK HOME?
I CALL MYSELF ***ALTUUM.***

MEANWHILE IN THE FINANCIAL DISTRICT...
SEND THEM OUT, THEN WE CAN OPEN A DIALOGUE! NO NEED TO MAKE THIS MORE COMPLICATED THAN IT ALREADY IS.
<KSSHT> WE WANT TO WORK WITH YOU!
DC YOU TRUST
POLICE
WHAT ARE WE DEALING WITH?
AT LEAST FIVE GUNMEN, AND THEY HAVE HOSTAGES. THEY'VE ALREADY PROVEN THAT THEY'RE WILLING TO KILL.
WE'RE ON BORROWED TIME--
I'M GOING IN. WAIT FOR MY SIGNAL.
BY ALL MEANS!
BRAKKA BRAK KRAK
PIKT
TING
SKITT
BRAKKA KAKKA BRAAK
TING
TING
VIPP
VIPP
VIPP
BRAKKA KAKKA BRAAK
SPANG

KRAKKA KRAK
THEY CALLED IN WONDER WOMAN?!
--WE GOTTA PULL OUT!
SHE DIED ONCE, SHE CAN DO IT AGAIN!
IF IT REALLY *IS* WONDER WOMAN, SHE WON'T DO ANYTHING AS LONG AS WE HAVE *HOSTAGES.*
KRAKKA KRAKKA KRAK
BRAKKA BRAKKA BRAKKA
SHE HAS A MORAL *CODE.*
WE CAN USE THAT AGAINST HER.
TING
TING
TING
SHATHOOM
PUT THE GUNS DOWN AND SPARE YOURSELVES.
I HAVE SOMEWHERE TO BE, AND I'M ALREADY LATE.

BRRRRAPPPP-BRAP-BRAP
SO BE IT.
WHEN THIS IS OVER, REMEMBER--I OFFERED YOU MERCY.
TING
TING
TING
TING
TING
SHLACK
WHA-- WHAT THE--!
TING TING TING
UNGH!
FWIPP
SAVE YOUR BULLETS.
THESE GUNS WILL NOT SERVE YOU, JUST AS THEY WON'T STOP ME.

I'M SORRY, MAN! I CAN'T--!
TRAITOR! WE HAD A PLAN!
NO HONOR AMONG THIEVES? NOW THERE'S A SURPRISE.
BRRRRAAPPPP
YOU WOULD KILL ONE OF YOUR OWN--A PUNISHMENT FOR HIS COWARDICE?
UNNGH!
I WILL TEACH YOU COMPASSION...
...THEN YOU WILL UNDERSTAND WHY HE RAN.

--I SPEND MOST OF MY TIME ALONE. I RARELY VISIT THE MAINLAND.
I'M WHAT YOU MAY CALL, AND FORGIVE ME IF I MISAPPLY THE PHRASE...
...A *SOLE SURVIVOR.*
SLIIIP

I THINK YOU MEAN YOU'RE AN *INTROVERT.*
BUT IN A WAY WE'RE *ALL* SURVIVORS. EVERY DAY IS A STRUGGLE, AND BLESS EACH OF US FOR GETTIN' THROUGH.

AH, YES. FORGIVE ME, *ALGLAIS* IS NOT MY NATIVE TONGUE.
I AM GLAD YOU UNDERSTAND.

IF YOU DON'T MIND ME ASKING, WHAT *IS* YOUR FIRST LANGUAGE?
I CAN'T QUITE PLACE YOUR *ACCENT--*

OOP! EXCUSE ME, I GOTTA GRAB THIS.

HEY! YES-- YEAH, OF COURSE.
I CAN BE THERE IN FIFTEEN, IF YOU DON'T MIND WAITING.
SURE.
SEE YA THEN.

AT THAT VERY MOMENT...
I PROPOSE WE RESOLVE THIS NOW, WITHOUT ANY FURTHER VIOLENCE.
OF COURSE, IF YOU'D RATHER MAKE IT SWIFT *AND* PAINFUL, I CAN DO THAT TOO.

GRAB ME WITH THAT WHIP, AND IT'S THE LAST THING SHE SEES!

WRONG CHOICE.

P...PLEASE...

BRAK

GOT YOU.
TING
TING
FOR MONEY?
ALL THIS, FOR MONEY?
SHA-KLAK
I'VE FACED DOWN MONSTERS, GODS--BEINGS OF PURE ENERGY!
YET YOU STILL THINK YOU CAN BEST ME? FOOLISH DOESN'T BEGIN TO DESCRIBE YOUR DECISIONS!
PING
TING
TING
YOU HAVE SOWN SEEDS OF PAIN-- NOW REAP YOUR OWN MISERY.
KRAK
GULP

YOU.
...WHAT TIME IS IT?
UHH, TWO... FORTY...
I AM VERY LATE.
KA-KRAK
NO--NO, PLEASE! I'LL DO ANYTHING!
TOO LATE.
THE TIME FOR DIPLOMACY HAS COME TO AN END!
CRASH

SHOULD WE GO IN? OR...
NO! WE WAIT FOR HER SIGNAL--
DC YOU. TRUST
THAT, UH...MUST BE IT, THEN.
WHUMP
WHOOOAAA--!
WHUD
UNGHH--
THIS IS THE LAST OF THEM. SEE TO IT THAT THE HOSTAGES GET MEDICAL ATTENTION.
I'M SORRY I CAN'T STICK AROUND...

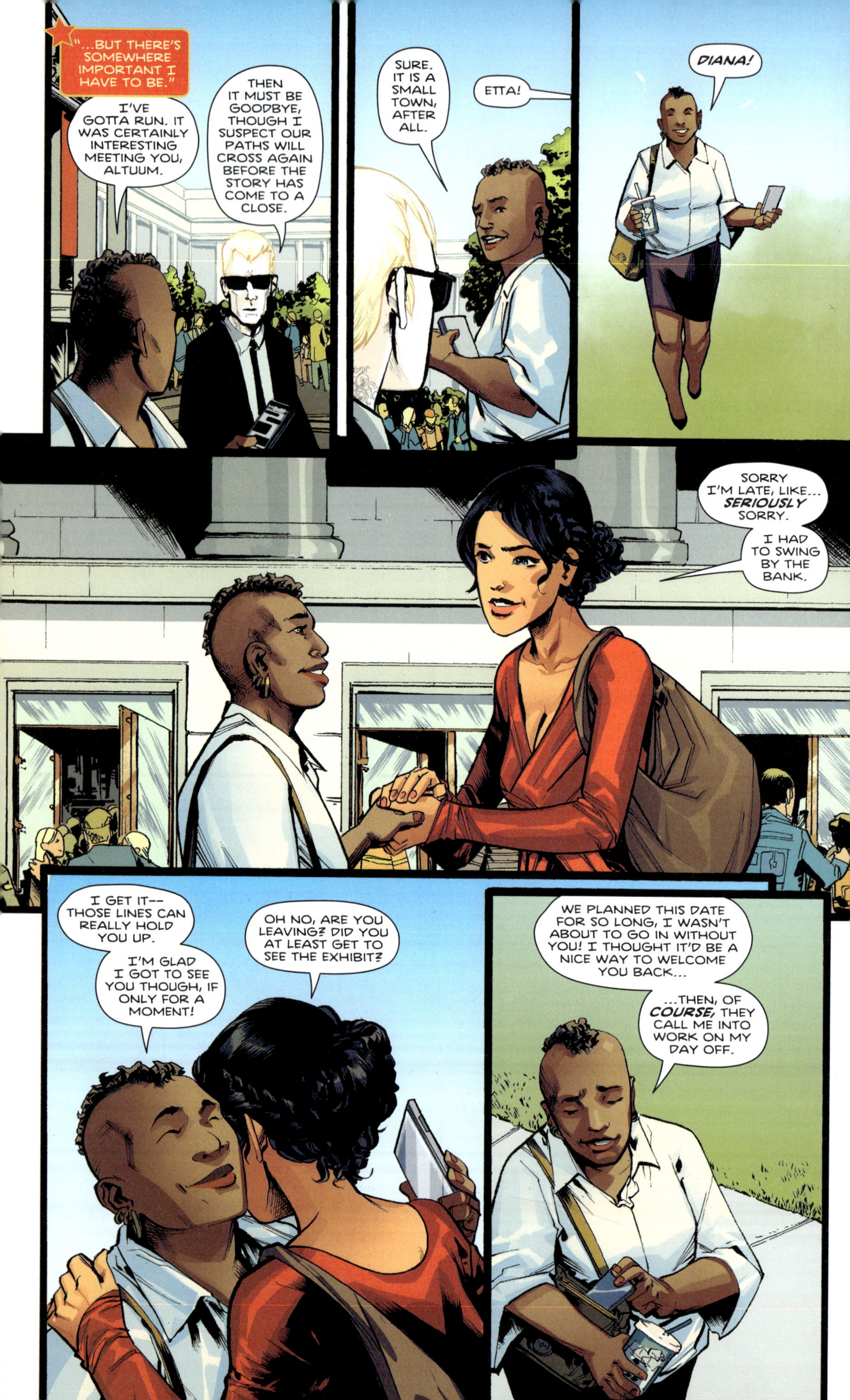
"...BUT THERE'S SOMEWHERE IMPORTANT I HAVE TO BE."
I'VE GOTTA RUN. IT WAS CERTAINLY INTERESTING MEETING YOU, ALTUUM.
THEN IT MUST BE GOODBYE, THOUGH I SUSPECT OUR PATHS WILL CROSS AGAIN BEFORE THE STORY HAS COME TO A CLOSE.
SURE. IT IS A SMALL TOWN, AFTER ALL.
ETTA!
DIANA!
SORRY I'M LATE, LIKE... SERIOUSLY SORRY.
I HAD TO SWING BY THE BANK.
I GET IT-- THOSE LINES CAN REALLY HOLD YOU UP.
I'M GLAD I GOT TO SEE YOU THOUGH, IF ONLY FOR A MOMENT!
OH NO, ARE YOU LEAVING? DID YOU AT LEAST GET TO SEE THE EXHIBIT?
WE PLANNED THIS DATE FOR SO LONG, I WASN'T ABOUT TO GO IN WITHOUT YOU! I THOUGHT IT'D BE A NICE WAY TO WELCOME YOU BACK...
...THEN, OF COURSE, THEY CALL ME INTO WORK ON MY DAY OFF.

THEY CAN'T DO THAT, CAN THEY?
IT'S UNFAIR!
⩥SIGH⩤ IT REALLY IS. AT LEAST I GOT TO ENJOY SOME TIME IN THE SUN BEFORE HEADING BACK TO THE DINGY OL' OFFICE!
ETTA, NO! NEXT TIME I SWEAR I'LL BE ON TIME.
STOP APOLOGIZING!
I CAN'T HELP IT. WE NEVER GET ENOUGH TIME TOGETHER, JUST US.
I KNOW-- BUT WE CAN'T HELP THAT WE'RE VERY IN-DEMAND, CAN WE?
BRUNCH SOON, YEAH?
YEAH.
SOON.
AGAIN... I'M SORRY--
GIRL, STOP! I KNOW A GOOD SPOT. JUST CALL ME WHEN YOU'RE FREE.
NOW GO-- ENJOY THE EXHIBIT! YOU CAN TELL ME ALL ABOUT IT OVER BRUNCH.
THAT ETTA CANDY...
SHE REALLY IS TOO GOOD TO ME.

SHE IS A TRUE FRIEND. WHEN SHE SUGGESTED WE TAKE A DAY OFF TO SEE THIS EXHIBIT, I ALMOST LAUGHED.

I MEAN, WHEN DO WE EVER GET DAYS OFF?

MORE THAN THAT THOUGH, WHY GO TO AN EXHIBIT ABOUT MY ISLAND WHEN WE COULD SIMPLY VISIT AND SEE THE ***REAL THING?***

THEMYSCIRA

THROUGH A LIFTING FOG

BUT THAT WAS AN UNFAIR THING TO THINK.

Art and artifacts inspired by and collected from the mysterious homeland of the once-deceased hero Wonder Woman. Never-before-seen photographs, artisitic interpretations, and relics of the Amazonian "Paradise Island."

Presented by the MOAH, in cooperation with the Amazon Embassy, a celebration of Themysciran culture through the ages

ETTA IS INTERESTED IN WHERE I COME FROM-- THE AMAZONS, OUR HISTORY AND CULTURE.
NOW THAT I'M HERE, I UNDERSTAND HOW MUCH SHARING THIS MOMENT WOULD HAVE MEANT TO BOTH OF US.

THERE'S ALSO SOMETHING FASCINATING ABOUT SEEING THEMYSCIRA THROUGH THE LENS OF MAN'S WORLD...

...THOUGH I STILL THINK THIS WOULD HAVE BEEN A LOT MORE FUN WITH ETTA.
--AN ISLAND NO MAN HAS EVER SET FOOT ON, LONG THOUGHT TO BE MYTH, BUT NOW ACKNOWLEDGED BY THE SCIENTIFIC AND GEOLOGICAL COMMUNITIES TO, IN FACT, BE VERY REAL INDEED.
A PLACE PERHAPS BEST KNOWN AS THE ONCE HOME OF...
...WONDER WOMAN!
CLAP CLAP CLAP CLAP
PERHAPS YOU'VE SEEN HER IN THE NEWS RECENTLY?
BACK FROM THE DEAD AND WASTING NO TIME SAVING REFUGEES.
IT'S NO WONDER THEY CALL HER WONDER WOMAN!
HA HA HA HA!
WHEN SHE CAME TO WHAT THE AMAZONS REFER TO AS MAN'S WORLD GENERATIONS AGO, WE KNEW VERY LITTLE OF HER INTENTIONS.
THANKFULLY, TIME AND AGAIN WONDER WOMAN HAS PROVEN AN ALLY AGAINST TYRANNY, BECOMING AN ICON TO WOMEN, NONBINARY FOLKS, AND MEN ALIKE!
BY MAKING MAN'S WORLD HER HOME, SHE HAS HELPED TO TRANSFORM IT INTO OUR WORLD.
A PLACE WHERE, WHILE INEQUALITY STILL EXISTS...
...WE CAN JOIN HANDS AND HELP EACH OTHER THRIVE, TOGETHER.
Nevaeh

HERE WE FIND A PRINT OF THE FIRST PHOTOGRAPH EVER TAKEN OF WONDER WOMAN. A BIT FUZZY, BUT THIS HAS BEEN VERIFIED AS THE REAL THING!
THOSE WHO HAVE SEEN THE RECENT FOOTAGE OF HER HAVE TO BE WONDERING THE SAME THING I AM...
...WHAT IS HER *SKIN CARE* ROUTINE?!
HA HA HA HA!
CLAP CLAP CLAP CLAP
IT ISN'T FAIR, RIGHT?
HA HA HA HA!
CLAP CLAP CLAP
YEAH, ETTA WOULD HAVE *LOVED* THIS...
...AND SHE ALSO WOULD HAVE SAID SOMETHING TO THIS GUY WHO'S BEEN *TRAILING* ME SINCE I ARRIVED.
LIKE-- WHAT KINDA CONDITIONER ARE YOU USING?
HA HA HA!

AND WITH THAT, I'LL LEAVE YOU TO ENJOY THE SHOW.
THERE ARE PAMPHLETS AVAILABLE IN THE LOBBY, BUT I'LL STILL BE HERE TO ANSWER ANY OTHER QUESTIONS YOU MIGHT HAVE!
I TAKE IT YOU WISH TO SPEAK WITH ME?
IS MY INTENTION THAT APPARENT?
CONSIDERING YOU FOLLOWED ME HERE, AND HAVEN'T SEEMED AT ALL INTERESTED IN THE EXHIBIT SO FAR? I'D SAY SO.
OH, BUT I *DO* FIND THE EXHIBITION FASCINATING.
I CAME TO SEE *IT* AS MUCH AS I CAME HERE TO SEE YOU...
...*DIANA.*
I'M SORRY, HAVE WE *MET?*
NO. BUT WE ARE MEETING NOW.
AND I SUSPECT THAT WE WILL BOTH LEARN A GREAT DEAL, HAVING FINALLY SHARED A MOMENT.

YOUR MOTHER, I PRESUME?
TELL ME, DID THEY CAPTURE HER LIKENESS?
I DON'T SEE WHY I SHOULD KEEP SPEAKING WITH SOMEONE WHO HASN'T EVEN GIVEN ME HIS NAME.
MY APOLOGIES, I WENT AHEAD OF MYSELF.
I AM ALTUUM...
...THE *SURVIVOR.*
AND WHAT DO YOU KNOW OF MY MOTHER AND ME, ALTUUM?
AAAH, I KNOW MUCH OF YOUR *PEOPLE.*
FOR INSTANCE, THIS PAINTING IS TRYING TO DEPICT THE AMAZONIAN HARVEST OBSERVANCE.
HERE THEY CALL IT A *RITUAL,* BUT IT IS MORE OF AN ACT OF THANKSGIVING.
AN ECSTATIC TRIBUTE TO THE GODS...
...YOUR GODS.
THE ONES WHO GAVE YOU SUCH A PARADISE OF PLENTY.

YES, I AM WELL AWARE OF THE FESTIVAL, BUT YOUR UNDERSTANDING IS LIMITED.
THE DANCE IS TO CELEBRATE WHAT IS TO COME--OUR SHARED RESPONSIBILITY TO MAKE GOOD USE OF THE BOUNTY.
NOW IF YOU'LL EXCUSE ME...
THE ISLE IS FERTILE.
ITS HARVESTS HAVE ALWAYS BEEN GENEROUS.
THAT CANNOT BE TRUE.
YOU SPEAK AS IF YOU'VE BEEN.
YES.
YOU WOULD KNOW MORE ABOUT THE TRUTH THAN ANYONE. FACTS DO NOT CHANGE DEPENDING ON THE KNOWLEDGE ONE HAS ACCESS TO...
...THEY REMAIN STEADFAST.
BEHOLD.

THERE-- UNDER THE WAVES, JUST NORTH OF THE ISLE OF HEALING. *THAT* IS WHERE MY PEOPLE LIVE.
WE, THE ORIGINAL INHABITANTS OF THE ISLAND! THE ONES DISPLACED BY YOUR PEOPLE, LONG BEFORE HISTORY BEGAN.
...WHAT AM I LOOKING AT?
YOU'RE LOOKING AT OUR VESSEL! OUR HOME BENEATH THE WAVES! HIDDEN FAR BELOW THE SURFACE, AWAY FROM THE SUN, THE STARS--
A PLACE OF WAITING...

...AND OF WATCHING.

YOU'RE TELLING ME THAT'S A *SUBMARINE?*

AN OVER-SIMPLIFICATION...

...BUT *YES.*

YOU SAID YOU WERE WAITING.

FOR *WHAT,* EXACTLY?

FOR YOU TO *DIE,* NATURALLY.

WE CAN HANDLE THE OTHERS.

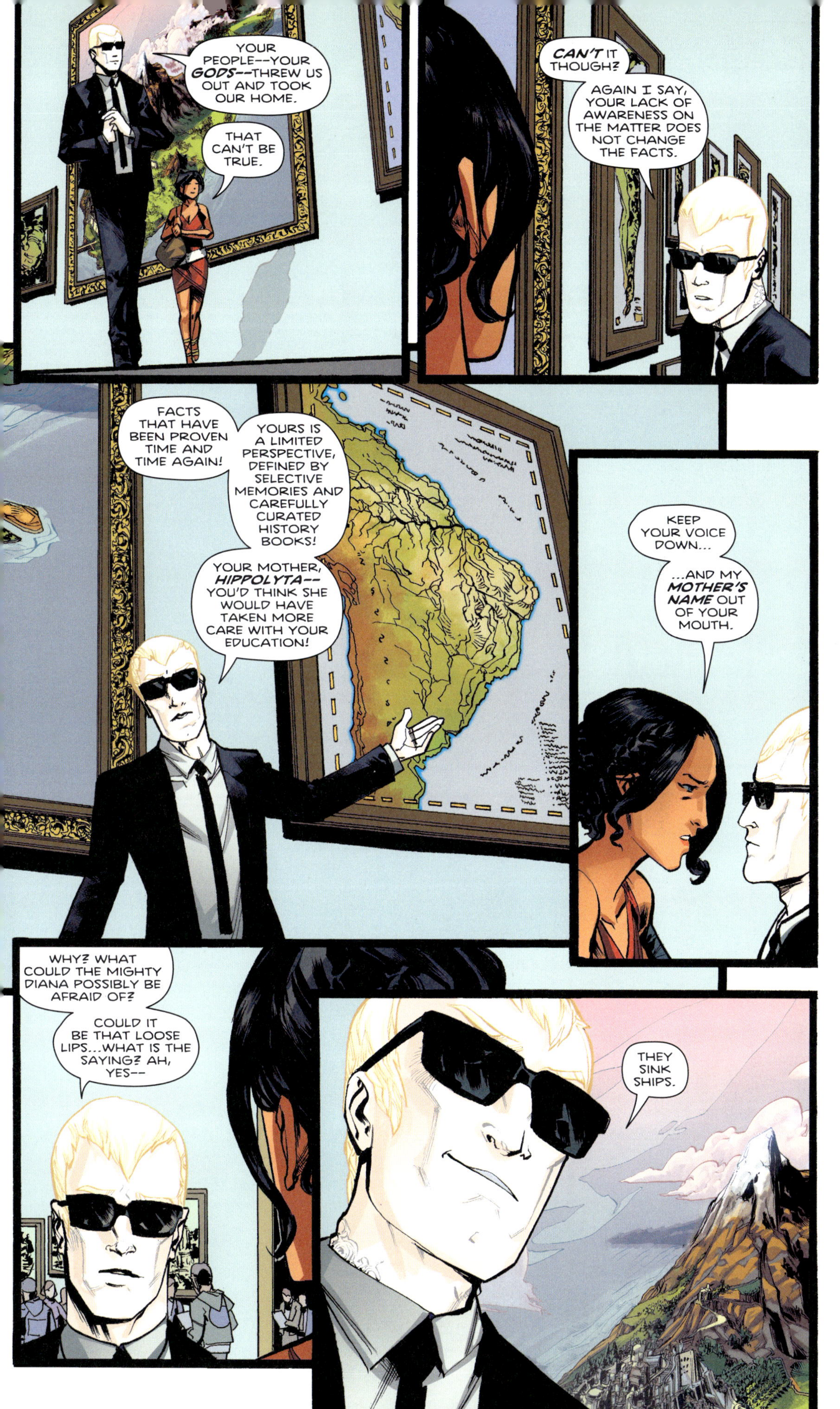
YOUR PEOPLE--YOUR GODS--THREW US OUT AND TOOK OUR HOME.
THAT CAN'T BE TRUE.
CAN'T IT THOUGH?
AGAIN I SAY, YOUR LACK OF AWARENESS ON THE MATTER DOES NOT CHANGE THE FACTS.
FACTS THAT HAVE BEEN PROVEN TIME AND TIME AGAIN!
YOURS IS A LIMITED PERSPECTIVE, DEFINED BY SELECTIVE MEMORIES AND CAREFULLY CURATED HISTORY BOOKS!
YOUR MOTHER, HIPPOLYTA-- YOU'D THINK SHE WOULD HAVE TAKEN MORE CARE WITH YOUR EDUCATION!
KEEP YOUR VOICE DOWN...
...AND MY MOTHER'S NAME OUT OF YOUR MOUTH.
WHY? WHAT COULD THE MIGHTY DIANA POSSIBLY BE AFRAID OF?
COULD IT BE THAT LOOSE LIPS...WHAT IS THE SAYING? AH, YES--
THEY SINK SHIPS.

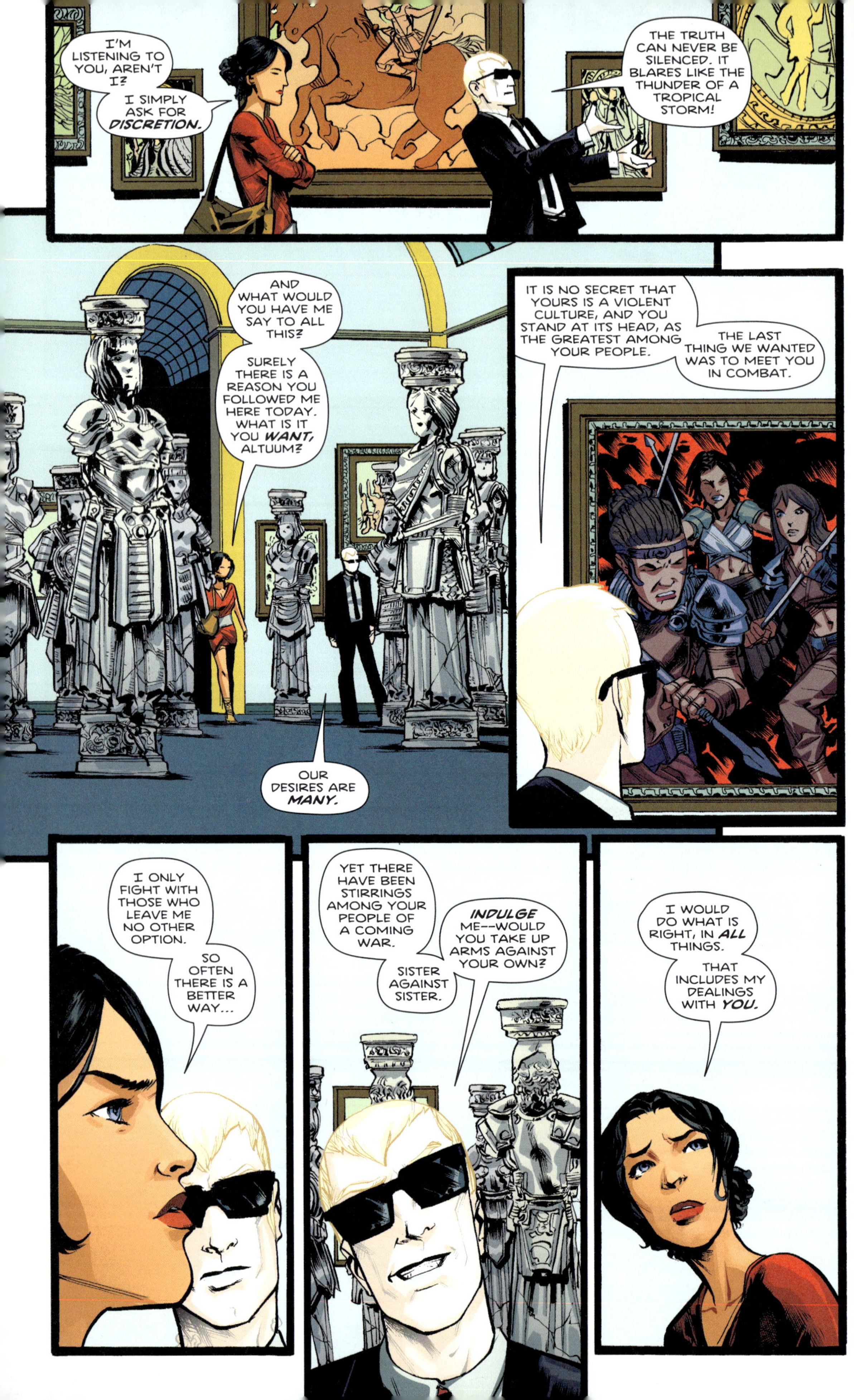

I'M LISTENING TO YOU, AREN'T I?
I SIMPLY ASK FOR ***DISCRETION.***
THE TRUTH CAN NEVER BE SILENCED. IT BLARES LIKE THE THUNDER OF A TROPICAL STORM!

AND WHAT WOULD YOU HAVE ME SAY TO ALL THIS?
SURELY THERE IS A REASON YOU FOLLOWED ME HERE TODAY. WHAT IS IT YOU ***WANT,*** ALTUUM?
OUR DESIRES ARE ***MANY.***

IT IS NO SECRET THAT YOURS IS A VIOLENT CULTURE, AND YOU STAND AT ITS HEAD, AS THE GREATEST AMONG YOUR PEOPLE.
THE LAST THING WE WANTED WAS TO MEET YOU IN COMBAT.

NOW I ASK YOU TO INDULGE ME.
YOU CHOSE TO HAVE THIS CONVERSATION IN PUBLIC, ON YOUR TERMS. CLEARLY THE GOAL WAS TO MAKE ME FEEL TRAPPED.
SO TELL ME-- WHAT KIND OF REACTION WERE YOU LOOKING FOR?
I SEEK NOTHING FROM YOU, TRULY. I SIMPLY WANT YOU TO KNOW.
YOU SAID SOME INTERESTING THINGS, AND AS YOU WANTED, I LISTENED.
HOWEVER, I'M LESS IMPRESSED WITH THE EVIDENCE YOU'VE PRESENTED.
YOUR SO-CALLED SHIP COULD JUST AS EASILY BE A CORAL REEF. THEN YOU CALL OUR ENTIRE HISTORY INTO QUESTION, WITH NO PROOF?
PERHAPS I WOULD HAVE BEEN MORE OPEN TO A DIALOGUE IF YOU HAD APPROACHED ME WITH SOME RESPECT.
EXIT
AS IT STANDS, YOU HAVEN'T GIVEN ME A SINGLE REASON TO BELIEVE YOU.
YOU SPEAK OF RESPECT, YET YOU WOULD TURN YOUR BACK ON ME?
I AM ALTUUM THE SURVIVOR!
YOU NEED NOT BELIEVE! THE ENKI PEOPLE SHALL RISE ALL THE SAME!

REMEMBER THIS MOMENT. YOUR ***FEAR*** WILL BE WHAT SEES YOU THROUGH THE DARKNESS THAT IS COMING.

YOU MAY BE STRONG...

...BUT YOUR READ ON THE SITUATION IS PROFOUNDLY INCORRECT.

DON'T MAKE A SCENE.

CLIK
BRRRRIIIIINGG
FIRE ALARM

FIRE!
EVERYONE! EVACUATE THE GALLERY, QUICKLY!
BRRRRIIIIINGG
DID YOU NOT HEAR WHAT I SAID?
AND YOU--TAKE YOUR HAND OFF OF ME!
UNGH!
THIS IS HOW YOU WISH IT TO BE?
YOU LEFT ME NO CHOICE.
SO BE IT.

WAR IS COMING, AMAZON. MAKE NO MISTAKE.
AND AFTER THEMYSCIRA BURNS TO THE GROUND, THE ENKI PEOPLE WILL RISE AGAIN AND RECLAIM OUR ANCESTRAL HOME.
YOU KNOW NOTHING OF THE AMAZONS...
...ALLOW ME TO GIVE YOU AN EDUCATION.
KLOCK
REMIND ME TO GRAB THOSE WHEN WE'RE DONE, AND I'LL HELP YOU FIND YOUR TEETH.
VERY WELL...

KRAK
I LISTENED, EVEN WHILE YOU THREATENED ME! NOW IT'S ***YOUR*** TURN TO HEAR ***ME*** OUT.

I WILL ***NOT*** BE MANHANDLED!
NOT BY YOU, NOT BY ***ANYONE!***
WHAT DID I SAY? THE AMAZONS ARE A VIOLENT PEOPLE--YOUR REACTION SIMPLY PROVES MY POINT.

YOUR PEOPLE ARE TOO PREOCCUPIED WITH WAR TO REALIZE THEIR PRECIOUS ISLAND SITS ON A POWDER KEG.
YOU STILL DO NOT KNOW WHAT HORRORS LURK ON THE OTHER SIDE OF ***DOOM'S DOORWAY.***

BUT I PROMISE YOU, AMAZON--YOU SHALL UNDERSTAND SOON ENOUGH!

WE ARE THE HEROES OF OUR PEOPLE, YOU AND I.

AND WHILE MY GODS ARE DEAD, AND MY PEOPLE FORCED INTO EXILE...

CRASH

...I REMAIN PREPARED TO DIE FOR THE ENKI IDEALS!

LET'S HOPE IT DOESN'T COME TO THAT, BECAUSE I REFUSE TO HOLD BACK FOR LONG.

I SHOULD HOPE NOT. WE'VE PREPARED FOR THOUSANDS OF YEARS TO FACE AN AMAZON CHAMPION.
I'D HATE FOR YOU TO DISAPPOINT ME!
SCWACK
FUNNY...
...THINKING YOU COULD PREPARE FOR ME.
THIS IS EXACTLY WHAT YOU WANTED, ISN'T IT? FROM THE MOMENT YOU FOLLOWED ME IN HERE...
WHACK
...YOU PROVOKED AND INSULTED ME, THREATENED MY SAFETY AND MY PEOPLE.
KRAK
I GAVE YOU A CHANCE...
...NOW WE DO THINGS MY WAY.

THIS WON'T HURT A BIT.
PERHAPS NOT FOR YOU, WONDER WOMAN...
...PERHAPS NOT FOR YOU.
WAIT--!
CLIK
KA-THOOM

BOOM
WEEE-OOOO WEEE-OOOO

RUN!
I CAN'T FIND MY BROTHER--
CALL 9-1-1! WE NEED AN AMBULANCE!
ARE THERE PEOPLE STILL INSIDE?!
NOBODY PANIC! IF YOU NEED MEDICAL HELP, COME THIS WAY!

WEEE-OOOO
WEEE-OOOO

ARE YOU HURT?
NO--I THINK...I THINK IT WAS A BOMB!

THERE'S MOVEMENT IN THERE--GEAR UP AND GET INSIDE!
MOVE IT! THAT BLAZE IS SPREADING FAST.
I WANT BOOTS IN AND OUT, NOW! WE'VE GOT A MAJOR COLLAPSE RISK!
DON'T SEND THEM IN, CAPTAIN.
THIS MAN NEEDS MEDICAL ATTENTION.
WONDER WOMAN...THANK YOU FOR YOUR HELP.
WE'LL TAKE IT FROM HERE.

DAYS LATER.
HERE YOU ARE, TWO OAT MILK FLAT WHITES!
THANK YOU.
SO...
HAVE YOU FOUND HIM YET?
NO...
...BUT IF THERE WAS A SMALL TRUTH IN WHAT HE SAID, HIDING IS SOMETHING THIS GUY DOES WELL.
I *KNEW* IT!
KNEW WHAT?
I KNEW HE WAS A CREEP. FROM THE MOMENT HE OPENED HIS MOUTH, I HAD A *HUNCH.*
SOME PEOPLE JUST EXUDE A FUNK, AND PICKING IT UP IS LIKE A KIND OF SIXTH SENSE.
I WASN'T BUYING HIS EUROPEAN-TOURIST ACT, NOT FOR ONE SECOND.
WAIT. YOU DON'T ACTUALLY BELIEVE HIS CRAP?
AT THIS POINT, I'M NOT SURE *WHAT* TO THINK.
I WASN'T HOLDING MUCH BACK, AND THE WORST PART...?

...I SUSPECT THAT HE *WAS.*

WHAT HE *WAS* IS A CREEP! DON'T LET THIS WEIRDO'S MIND GAMES GET UNDER YOUR SKIN.
BESIDES, WE HAVE *BETTER* THINGS TO TALK ABOUT.

LIKE HOW I AM JUST NOW FINDING OUT THERE'S A DOOR...
...TO *HELL,* RIGHT UNDER PARADISE ISLAND?
Y'ALL MIGHT NEED A NEW NICKNAME FOR THE PLACE, NOW THAT I KNOW *THAT* LITTLE CHESTNUT!

AND I STILL NEED TO HEAR MORE ABOUT THE *AFTERLIFE!*
LAST TIME WE TALKED, YOU WERE ABOUT TO TELL ME ABOUT A NEW FRIEND...

C'MON, DIANA. I *KNOW* YOU HAVE STORIES FOR ME.

OH, MAYBE ONE OR TWO...

SHOOT. SORRY-- I HAVE NO CLUE WHO THIS COULD BE...
BRRRRIIIIINGGGG

OOP, THERE *I* GO NOW!
WHERE IN THE HECK IS THAT THING? I SWEAR, THIS BAG HAS TOO MANY POCKETS.
BEEP

TAK TAK TAKKA TAK
TAKKA TAK TAK TAK TAKKA

ETTA, I'M SORRY, I--
NOT A WORD! I GOTTA RUN TOO.

ONE OF THESE DAYS I SWEAR, WE'LL HAVE A *PROPER* CATCH-UP.
OH, IT'LL HAPPEN. I *WANT* THOSE STORIES!
SHOULD WE TRY AGAIN ON FRIDAY?

THIRD TIME'S THE CHARM! SAME TIME, SAME PLACE.

OKAY, LADIES, WE'VE GOT THE BOHEMIAN BENEDICT, PUMPERNICKEL TOAST, A SIDE OF COUNTRY FRIES, TWO FRUIT SALADS, AND A--
HEY...

WHERE DID THEY...?

OH...!

HANK, DID YOU SEE WHERE THOSE LADIES WENT?

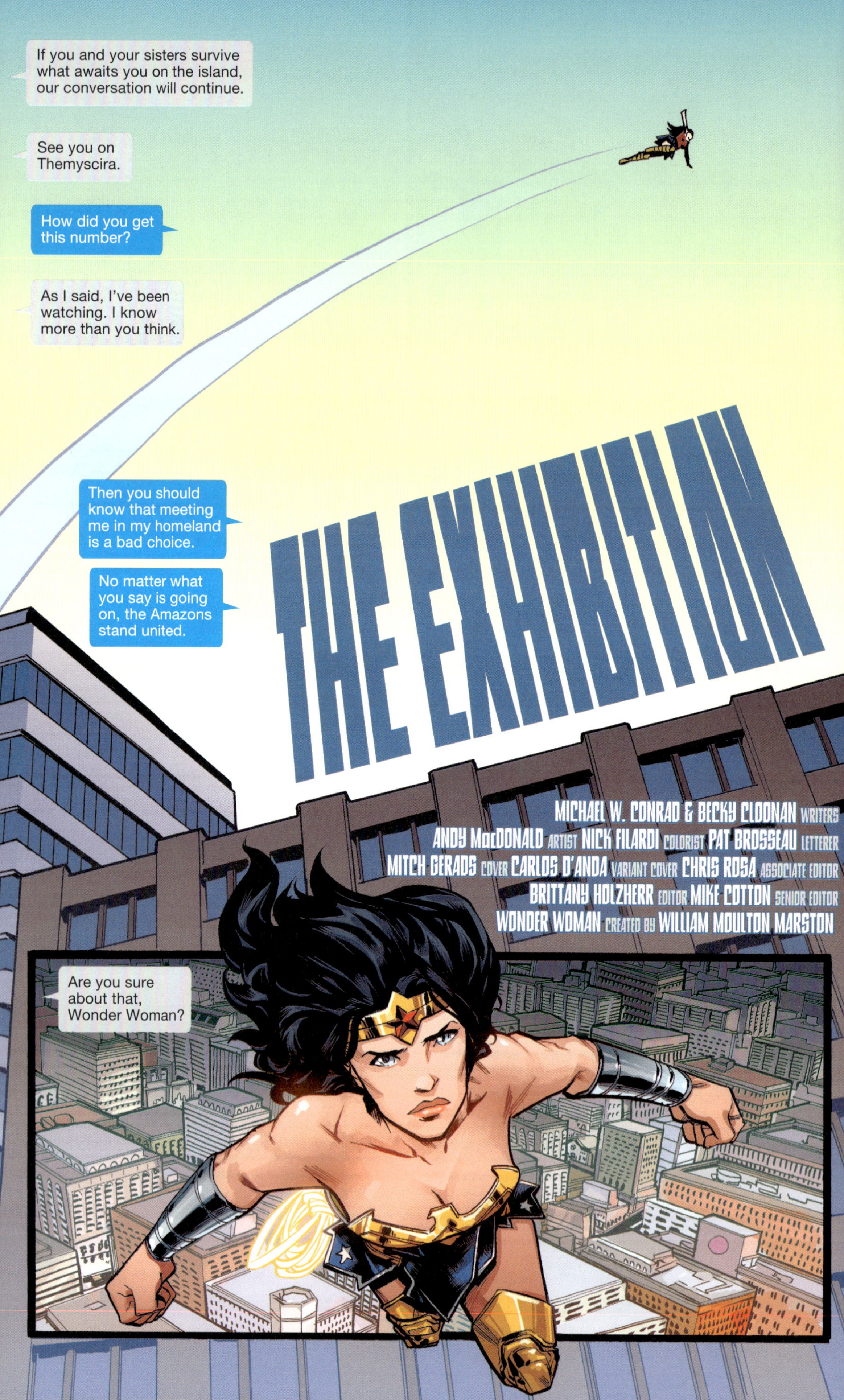
If you and your sisters survive what awaits you on the island, our conversation will continue.
See you on Themyscira.
How did you get this number?
As I said, I've been watching. I know more than you think.
Then you should know that meeting me in my homeland is a bad choice.
No matter what you say is going on, the Amazons stand united.
THE EXHIBITION
MICHAEL W. CONRAD & BECKY CLOONAN WRITERS
ANDY MacDONALD ARTIST NICK FILARDI COLORIST PAT BROSSEAU LETTERER
MITCH GERADS COVER CARLOS D'ANDA VARIANT COVER CHRIS ROSA ASSOCIATE EDITOR
BRITTANY HOLZHERR EDITOR MIKE COTTON SENIOR EDITOR
WONDER WOMAN CREATED BY WILLIAM MOULTON MARSTON
Are you sure about that, Wonder Woman?

***Wonder Woman* #781**
cover by TERRY DODSON
and RACHEL DODSON

***Wonder Woman* #781**
variant cover by WILL MURAI

WASHINGTON, D.C.
ROBBIN'S CAFE
OLYMPUS, ASGARD, ELFHAME...MOST OF US QUESTION WHERE WE GO AFTER OUR TIME ON EARTH IS UP--I FOUND THAT MY ANSWER WAS *MANY* PLACES.
I DON'T KNOW HOW ELSE TO DESCRIBE IT! AFTER COMING BACK HOME, THE WHOLE JOURNEY SEEMS...*SURREAL.*
HONEY, I CAN'T EVEN IMAGINE. LUCKY FOR ME I DON'T NEED TO!
WHEN MY TIME COMES, I PLAN TO LEAVE BROKE AND HAPPY. YOU WON'T CATCH ME COMIN' BACK!
TRINA'S
I'M NOT LIVIN' THE KINDA LIFE WHERE COMING BACK WOULD DO ANYONE ANY GOOD. BUT THEN AGAIN, I'M NOT...
...WONDER WOMAN.
ETTA *BETH* CANDY, I WOULD DEMAND YOUR RETURN!
EVEN IF I WOULD HAVE TO CARRY YOU BACK MYSELF!

AT LEAST WITH ME YOU WOULDN'T HAVE TO ANSWER ANY RIDDLES. YOU'D JUST HAVE TO CONVINCE ME THAT COMING BACK TO ALL THIS WOULD BE WORTH IT!

WELL...THERE ISN'T A SINGLE REALM IN THE SPHERE OF THE GODS THAT HAS A SALAD THIS DIVINE ON OFFER.
I MIGHT BE ABLE TO MAKE A CASE FOR MAN'S WORLD YET!

I MEAN... ETTA?
ARE YOU ALL RIGHT?
...WHAT IS HE DOING THERE?

DR. CIZKO?! WHO LET THAT MAN ON TELEVISION?
DR. EDGAR CIZKO: AUTHOR OF THE DELUSION KLTV STRAIGHT SHOOTERS LIVE
RING RIIIING

AND HE WROTE A BOOK?! HAVE I TRULY BEEN GONE THAT LONG?
RING RIIIING
SORRY, I GOTTA TAKE THIS-- HELLO?

YEAH, JUST FINISHING UP LUNCH. NO, NOT AT ALL.
OKAY, GREAT. NO, IT'S FINE! I'LL SEE YOU SOON. BYE!

THAT WAS STEVE.
OH! YOU'RE WORKING WITH HIM AGAIN?
YEAH. IT'S BEEN GOOD, BUT...ALWAYS BUSY! I GOTTA BE ON MY WAY.
WANT ME TO TELL HIM YOU SAID HI? YOU CAN'T AVOID HIM FOREVER.

I KNOW... AND I DON'T PLAN TO.
SEEING HIM AGAIN IS A PRIORITY, BUT THERE'S JUST SO MUCH RIGHT NOW THAT CAN'T BE PUT ON HOLD...

I FEEL AWFUL ASKING THIS OF YOU, BUT PLEASE, DON'T TELL HIM WE GOT TOGETHER.
I DON'T WANT HIM TO THINK I'M AVOIDING HIM...
NO, I UNDERSTAND. I WON'T SAY A WORD.

NOT LONG AFTER...
I'M NOT AVOIDING HIM. NOT ON PURPOSE.
SOMETHING ALWAYS COMES UP. IMPORTANT MATTERS THAT REQUIRE MY FULL ATTENTION.
KLTV
LIKE CATCHING UP WITH THE GOOD DOCTOR, FOR EXAMPLE. WE HAVE UNFINISHED BUSINESS.
SCREEECH
SCRUNCH
SPARE A MOMENT, CIZKO?

WELCOME HOME, DIANA.
I WISH I COULD SAY I'M HAPPY TO SEE YOU, BUT I KNOW HOW MUCH YOU LOATHE LYING.
WHAT CAN I DO TO MAKE YOU LEAVE?
VRRRRRRT

I HEAR YOU'RE AN AUTHOR NOW?
AH, SO YOU WANT MY AUTOGRAPH. THAT'LL BE FIFTY BUCKS.
WHAT I WANT IS AN EPILOGUE TO OUR LATEST CHAPTER.*
*SEE WONDER WOMAN VOL. 1: AFTERWORLDS! --BRITTANY

OH, LEAVE ME ALONE!
MY TIME IN ASGARD WAS BUT A DALLIANCE. IT HAD NOTHING WHATSOEVER TO DO WITH YOU! NOW SHOO.

I CAN SMELL YOUR SCHEMES FROM A MILE AWAY, AND WHATEVER YOU'RE DOING HERE? IT STINKS. REMEMBER...

...JUSTICE ISN'T A DISH YOU CAN SERVE COLD.
WHEN I CRUSH YOU UNDER MY HEEL, IT WILL BE WELL DESERVED--AND GARNISHED WITH THE RECENT MEMORIES OF YOUR FOUL DEEDS.
YOU'RE ON BORROWED TIME, DOCTOR.

OH, I'M ON BORROWED TIME, AM I?!
REMEMBER, *I'M* NOT THE ONE WHO WAS KILLED! AND IF IT CAN HAPPEN *ONCE...*
I'M NOT GOING ANYWHERE.

YOU TALK A GOOD GAME, TOOTS, BUT I'M THE *REAL DEAL.*
MEN ACROSS THE WORLD ARE TIRED OF YOUR POSTURING, AND I'M GIVING THEM A VOICE.
YOU'RE AS GOOD AS DONE.

YOU KNOW AS WELL AS I DO THAT YOUR VOICE IS JUST PANDERING TO A BIASED AUDIENCE.
NO MATTER HOW TWISTED YOUR GAMES, THE *TRUTH* WILL ALWAYS UNRAVEL THEM.

QUICK! SOMEBODY-- OH MY GOD, *HELP!*
HEAR THAT? THEY'RE PLAYING YOUR SONG. GO ON, RUN ALONG NOW.
BYE-BYE.
VRRRRRRT

GET US OUT OF HERE!
DRIVE!
SKREEEEE

WHOOSH

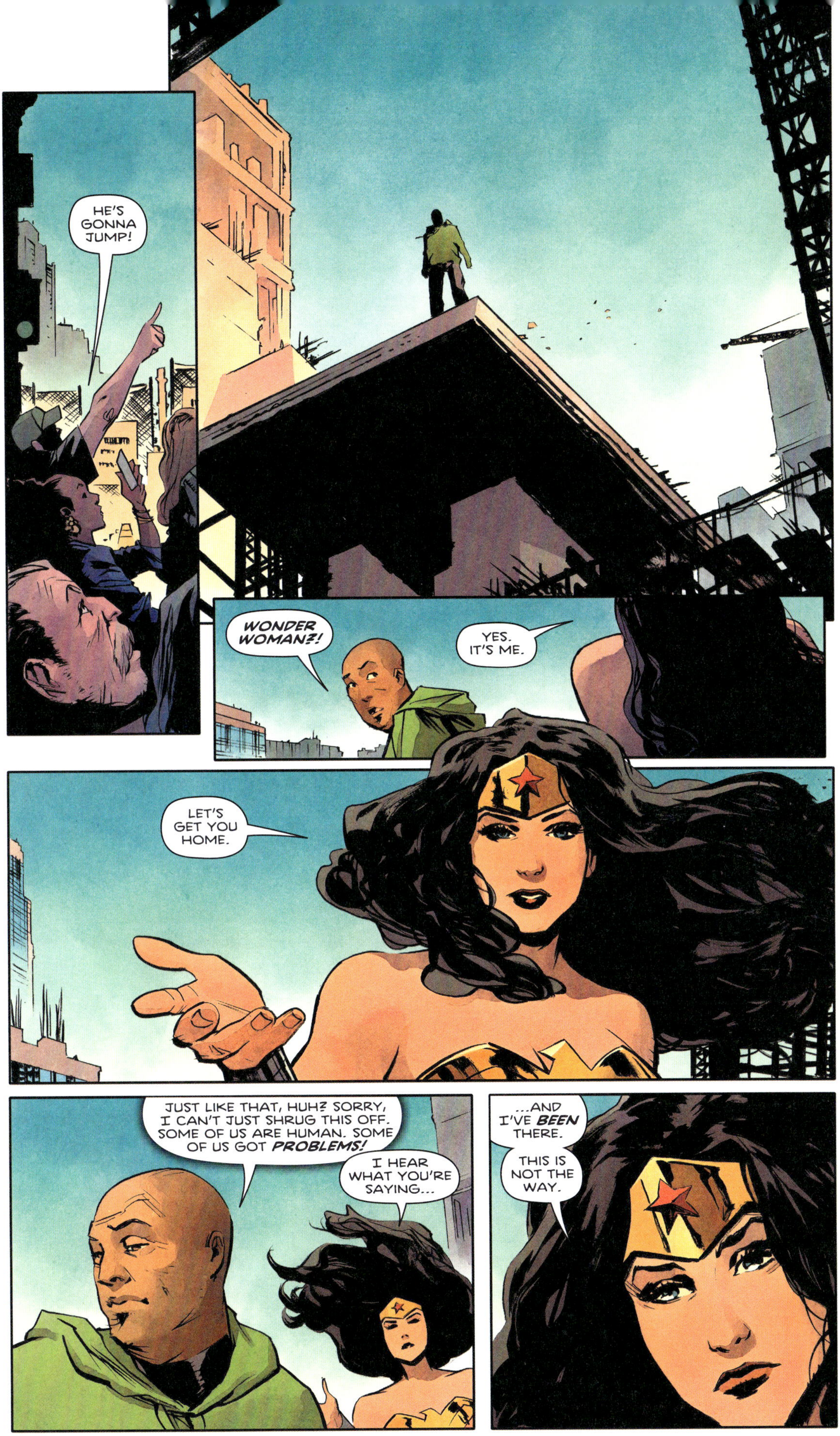

HE'S GONNA JUMP!

WONDER WOMAN?!

YES. IT'S ME.

LET'S GET YOU HOME.

HAH! IS THAT REALLY HOW YOU TALK A MAN OFF THE LEDGE?
IMMORTAL WONDER WOMAN'S BEEN THERE? YOU INSENSITIVE COW!

CIZKO.
LET THIS MAN GO. YOUR ANTICS WILL PROVE NOTHING.

WON'T THEY? TA-TA, DIANA!

SNAP

I'M COMING FOR YOU, CIZKO.
USE YOUR PARLOR TRICKS ALL YOU WISH, I'LL ALWAYS BE THERE TO STOP YOU.

AND WHAT IF I MAKE THE REST OF THESE HARD HATS JUMP? I KNOW YOU CAN'T SAVE THEM ALL.

SO YES. THIS IS A THREAT, DIANA.
STAY OUT OF MY BUSINESS, OR IT'S SPLAT, SPLAT, SPLAT...

OH GOD-- WHAT'S GOING ON? WHAT--

WONDER WOMAN?!
DON'T WORRY. I'VE GOT YOU...

NICE PLACE. IS IT YOURS?

YOU THINK I CAN SWING *THIS?*

I'M *DEAD.* THERE'S NOT A TON OF WORK FOR ME OUTSIDE OF ORGAN DONATION, AND MEDICAL-CADAVER GIGS. I CAN'T COMPLAIN, THOUGH. ESPECIALLY WHEN SO MANY HOUSES ARE LEFT VACANT.

YOU KNOW-- GRANDMA DIES, AND SUDDENLY YOU'RE RESPONSIBLE FOR HER ESTATE. BUT KIDS AND WORK KEEP YOU FROM SORTING IT OUT, SO YOU LET IT SIT...

...NEXT THING YOU KNOW, IT'S *HAUNTED!*

SO...CAN I GET YOU A DRINK?

THANK YOU, BUT NO.

IT'S *GOOD* TO SEE YOU, BOSTON.

SO GOOD. IT FEELS LIKE ONLY YESTERDAY WE WERE RIPPING IT UP IN THE SPHERE OF THE GODS!
HEY, YOUR SCAR! THE ONE JANUS GAVE YOU--IT'S GONE?
HM?

OH-- YES, I SUPPOSE IT IS.
HONESTLY, I HADN'T EVEN NOTICED. COMING BACK HAS BEEN...WELL, YOU KNOW.

I DO... IF YOU EVER NEED TO TALK, I'M HERE.
THANK YOU. IT'S ALL BEEN A BLUR.
SAYING HELLO TO PEOPLE WHO HAVE ALREADY SAID THEIR FAREWELLS...DON'T GET ME WRONG, I'M GLAD TO BE ALIVE.
IT'S JUST... A LOT OF EMOTIONS TO PROCESS.

I IMAGINE YOU'VE HAD TO MAKE YOUR FAIR SHARE OF GOODBYES AS WELL.

GRAM. SIEGFRIED WANTED ME TO HAVE IT, BUT I FEEL LIKE I'M HOLDING ON TO MORE THAN JUST A SWORD.
I'D LIKE TO RETURN IT. I THINK I'D FEEL MORE AT PEACE IF I KNEW HIS BLADE WAS RESTING CLOSE TO HIM.
THIS IS WHY I'VE COME TO YOU. CALL IT UNFINISHED BUSINESS.

ANY IDEAS?

LET'S SEE WHAT WE HAVE HERE.
HMM... IRON BLADE. GETTING A TRACE READING...

OOOM OOOM

OOOM
OOOOM
OOOM

OOOOMM

GASP

I THINK I'VE FOUND IT.
FOUND WHAT?
HIS BODY. WHAT **REMAINS** OF IT, ANYWAY.

HIS BODY? I MEAN, I KNOW SIGGY IS LONG DEAD...
I'M JUST SURPRISED YOU FOUND IT SO QUICKLY!
IT'S NOT AN EXACT SCIENCE, SO IT'S HARD TO BE SURE. I FOUND A PLACE THAT HIS BLADE HAS A SIGNIFICANT TETHER TO, IN ANY CASE.
YOU CAN BRING THE SWORD THERE...

...UNLESS YOU WANT TO GO BACK TO ASGARD?
HISTORICAL MAPS OF SCANDINAVIA

HAH! NO, OF COURSE--DEFINITELY NOT. I'VE SPENT ENOUGH TIME AWAY.
IT'S DECIDED, THEN. I WILL BRING THE SWORD TO HIS RESTING PLACE.

WE, ACTUALLY.
THIS SWORD IS SO OLD IT DOESN'T CARRY MUCH OF A SIGNAL ANYMORE. I NEED TO GET CLOSER TO THE SOURCE TO HOME IN ON THE LOCATION.
GUESS YOU'RE STUCK WITH ME AGAIN!

I CAN IMAGINE WORSE FATES.
SO, WHERE ARE WE GOING?

SOMEWHERE AROUND HERE.
BETTER PACK A JACKET, BOSTON.

WASHINGTON, D.C. THAT EVENING.
SHE'S BEEN BACK FOR A FEW DAYS NOW. STILL NO CALL.
SHE'S EITHER AVOIDING ME, OR...
DIANA?!
YES--I AM SHE. I AM WONDER WOMAN.

YOU CAME! I WAS BEGINNING TO THINK...
I AM WONDER WOMAN.
HURK!
I AM SHE.
CRASH
UGH!
WHAT THE HELL ARE YOU?
I AM WONDER WOMAN.

FWUMP
UNGH!
CRASH
STOP!
KRAK
BLAM

DIANA, I DON'T KNOW IF YOU HAVE A NEW PHONE YET, OR IF THIS NUMBER EVEN WORKS ANYMORE.
BUT IT'S ME, ANGEL...
...WE NEED TO TALK.

ELSEWHERE.
KNOCK KNOCK
KNOCK KNOCK
WHO KNOCKS?
IT'S ME. OPEN UP.
ME WHO? THIS SOME KINDA PRANK?
I'M RIGHT HERE, YOU DULLARD!
NOW OPEN THIS DOOR!

WHAT ARE YOU, LIVING IN A DICKENS NOVEL? INSTALL A BLASTED PEEPHOLE ALREADY!
APOLOGIES, DOCTOR.
I *COUGH* I HAVE PROCURED THE ITEM YOU REQUESTED. HAVE YOU BROUGHT ME SOMETHING TASTY TO EAT?

IT'S ALL THERE. NOW GIVE ME THE ARTIFACT, AND I'LL BE ON MY WAY.

I DIDN'T HAVE THE RIGHT CASE FOR IT, BUT YOU'LL FIND--
MY FRIEND, THIS IS THE REAL DEAL. TRUST ME.
YOUR SERVICES CAME **HIGHLY** RECOMMENDED, SO I TRUST YOU'RE NOT GOING TO STIFF ME.

PLEASURE DOING BUSINESS, THEN.

OH, THE PLEASURE WAS ALL--
WHAT IN THE...

THE DIRTY, ROTTEN CROOK!

GET BACK HERE! HEY, WHERE--?!
SONOVA...

MEANWHILE...
REMIND ME AGAIN WHY WE'RE TAKING A PLANE?
I NEED SOME TIME TO SIT WITH MY THOUGHTS, AND A NINE-HOUR FLIGHT WILL ALLOW ME TO DO JUST THAT.

--DO YOU ALWAYS DRESS LIKE A VAMPIRE?
DANG, I WAS GOING FOR JAMES DEAN BY WAY OF MARY SHELLEY.
I'M JUST THINKING, WE COULD HAVE TRAVELED, YOU KNOW-- THE QUICK WAY. SPLURGE ON A NICE HOTEL, BINGE SOME *MURDER FILES*...
EVER NOTICE THERE'S ALWAYS A *MURDER FILES* MARATHON WHEN YOU STAY IN A HOTEL?

SOMETIMES THERE IS COMFORT IN LETTING SOMEONE ELSE TAKE CONTROL FOR A MOMENT.
I HEAR YOU.
WONDER IF THEY HAVE ANYTHING TASTY ON THE MENU?

CHICKEN?
GREEN BEANS?!
NOW I SEE WHY YOU LIKE AIRPLANES.
HA HA! WHY, BOSTON, I DIDN'T REALIZE YOU WERE SUCH A GOURMAND.

THERE'S A LOT YOU DON'T KNOW ABOUT ME, MADEMOISELLE.

YOU KNOW, STEVE WAS A PILOT. MAYBE THAT'S WHY I FEEL SO COMFORTABLE UP HERE.
AH, YEAH. I DIDN'T EVEN THINK OF THAT. MAKES SENSE.

I DON'T KNOW WHY, BUT...I'M NERVOUS TO SEE HIM.

HE PROBABLY THINKS I'M AVOIDING HIM TOO. I'M DISAPPOINTED IN MYSELF. THIS ISN'T *LIKE* ME.
HEY, BEING DEAD ISN'T EASY--AND COMING BACK TO LIFE? WHEW.
DON'T BE SO HARD ON YOURSELF. YOU'RE ALLOWED TO TAKE WHATEVER TIME YOU NEED TO WORK THROUGH YOUR FEELINGS.

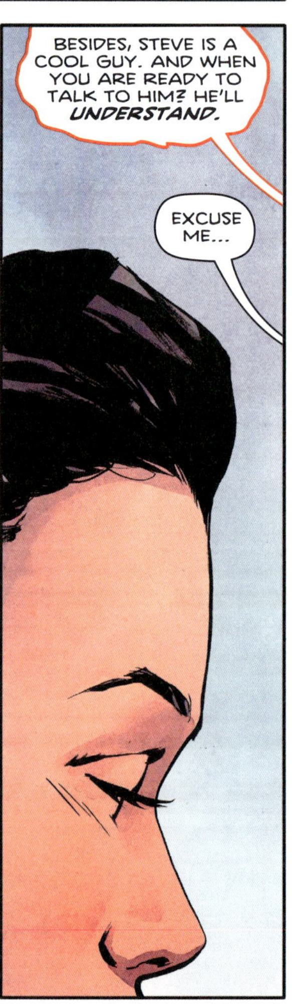
BESIDES, STEVE IS A COOL GUY. AND WHEN YOU ARE READY TO TALK TO HIM? HE'LL *UNDERSTAND.*
EXCUSE ME...

HERE YOU GO! ONE CHICKEN, AND ONE HUMMUS PLATTER.
WHAT KIND OF DRINKS WOULD YOU LIKE?
OH, *THANK* YOU! I CAN'T WAIT TO DIG IN.
I'LL TAKE A SPARKLING WATER...DIANA?

DIANA? YOU OKAY?

YEAH, ONLY...
I THOUGHT I SAW...
WHAT DO YOU MEAN?

I THINK THERE'S SOMETHING OUT THERE.
THROUGH A GLASS DARKLY
PART ONE
MICHAEL W. CONRAD & BECKY CLOONAN WRITERS
MARCIO TAKARA ARTIST TAMRA BONVILLAIN COLORIST
PAT BROSSEAU LETTERER TERRY DODSON & RACHEL DODSON COVER
WILL MURAI VARIANT COVER BRITTANY HOLZHERR EDITOR
MIKE COTTON SENIOR EDITOR
WONDER WOMAN CREATED BY WILLIAM MOULTON MARSTON

Wonder Woman #782
cover by TERRY DODSON
and RACHEL DODSON

***Wonder Woman* #782**
variant cover by WILL MURAI

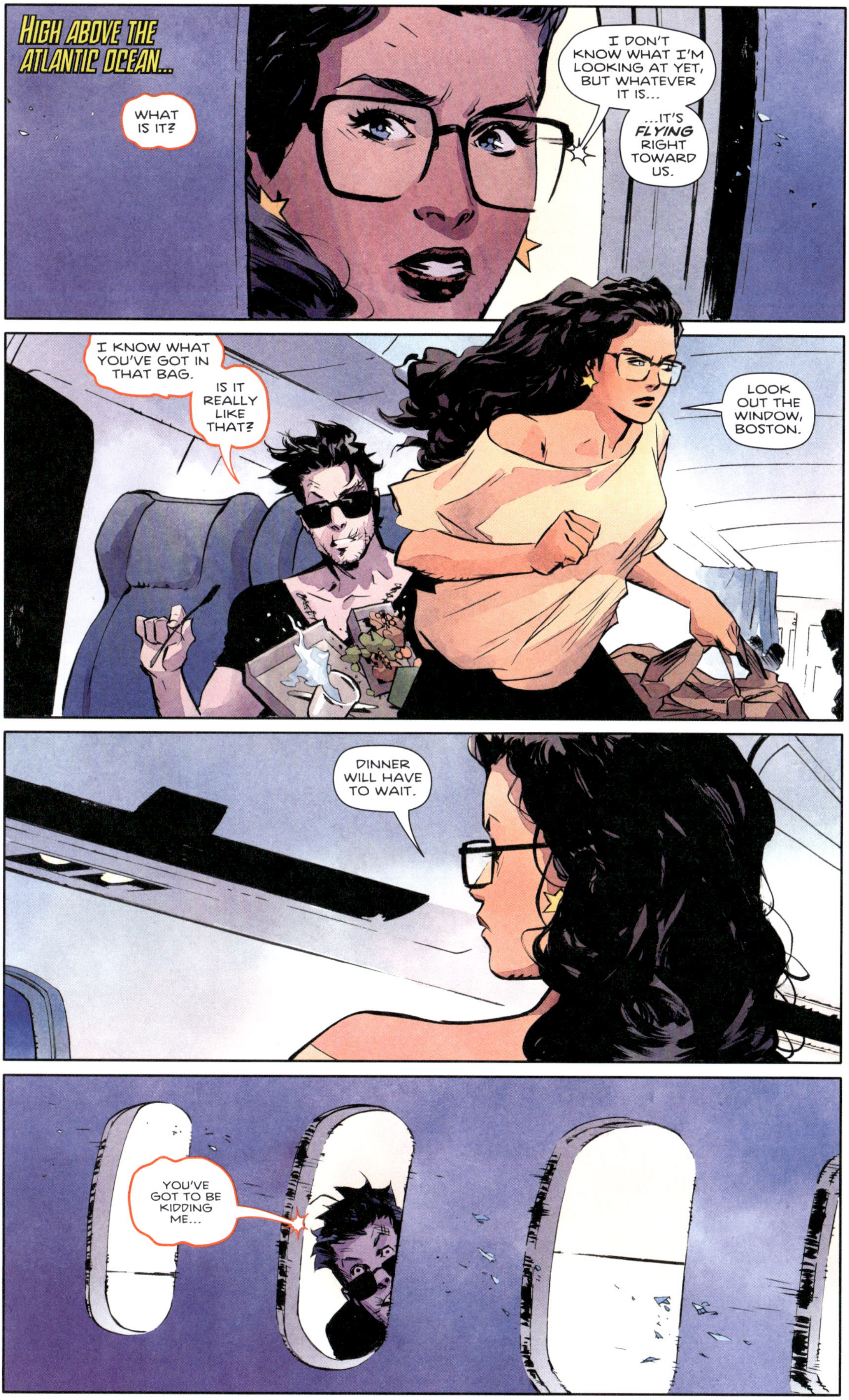

HIGH ABOVE THE ATLANTIC OCEAN...

WHAT IS IT?

I DON'T KNOW WHAT I'M LOOKING AT YET, BUT WHATEVER IT IS...

...IT'S ***FLYING*** RIGHT TOWARD US.

I KNOW WHAT YOU'VE GOT IN THAT BAG.

IS IT REALLY LIKE THAT?

LOOK OUT THE WINDOW, BOSTON.

DINNER WILL HAVE TO WAIT.

YOU'VE GOT TO BE KIDDING ME...

SORRY TO INTERRUPT YOUR IN-FLIGHT MEAL, BUT THINGS ARE ABOUT TO GET UGLY.
EXCUSE ME, SIR. YOU CAN'T JUST--
UM... I'M AN AIR MARSHAL!

SHEEE-KRUNK
NO MATTER WHAT HAPPENS NEXT, PLEASE, REMAIN CALM. AND REMEMBER--KEEP YOUR SEAT BELTS BUCKLED!
WHOOSH

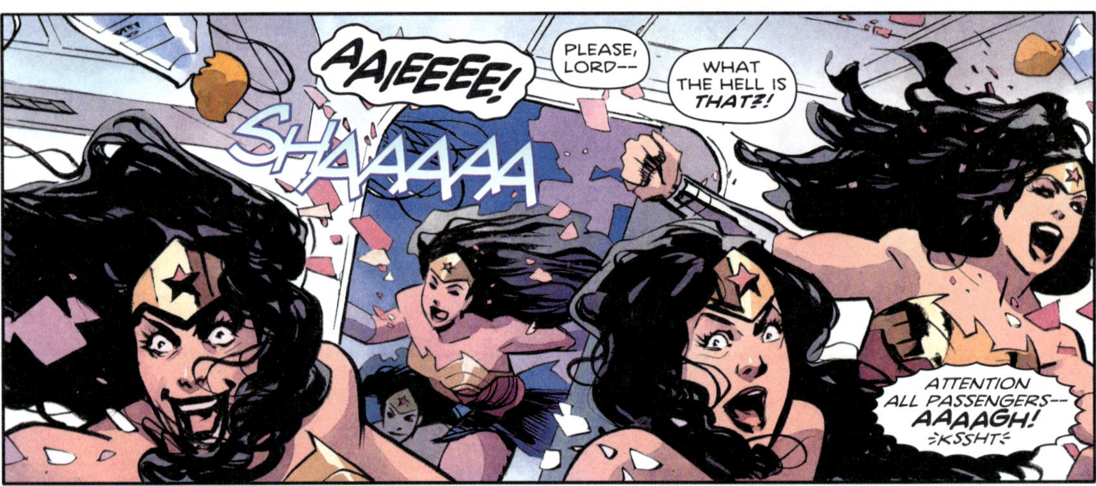
AAIEEEE!
SHAAAAAA
PLEASE, LORD--
WHAT THE HELL IS THAT?!
ATTENTION ALL PASSENGERS-- AAAAGH! KSSHT

PLEASE, TAKE MY SEAT!
WHAT ARE THESE THINGS? THEY LOOK LIKE--

I AM WONDER WOMAN.

NO YOU'RE NOT!
KLASH
...UH, SORRY?!

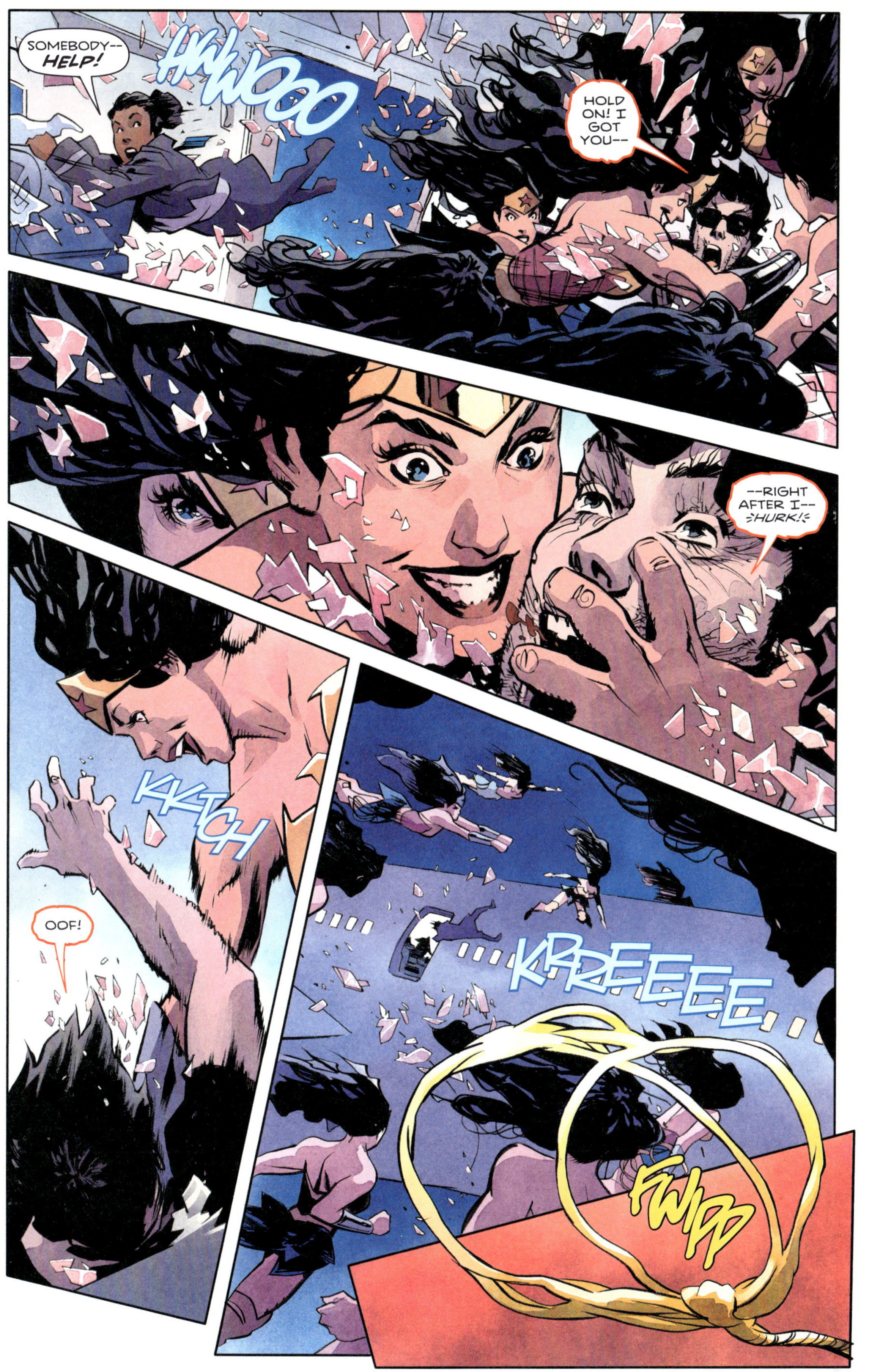
SOMEBODY-- HELP!
HWWOOO
HOLD ON! I GOT YOU--
--RIGHT AFTER I-- HURK!
KKTCH
OOF!
KRREEEEE
FWIDD

GREAT HERA, THAT WAS CLOSE!
SMASH
CRACK
RIGHT ON TIME!
WHAT IN HADES?
THEY SHATTER...!
I AM SHE.
I AM WONDER WOMAN.
THEY KEEP SAYING THAT!
THEY MAY BE WEAK, BUT THEY'RE MANY.
ENOUGH TO BRING THIS PLANE DOWN.
CRACK
SMASH

THESE THINGS HAVE NO LIFE SIGNS-- THEY'RE *GLASS!*
I'M WORKSHOPPING A JOKE ABOUT HOW THEY'RE NOT ALL THEY'RE CRACKED UP TO BE. IN THE MEANTIME, ANY CLUE WHAT THEY ARE?
YEAH.
THEY'RE *CHEAP COPIES!*
KSSSHH
THROUGH A GLASS DARKLY PART TWO
MICHAEL W. CONRAD & BECKY CLOONAN WRITERS
MARCIO TAKARA ARTIST TAMRA BONVILLAIN COLORIST
PAT BROSSEAU LETTERER TERRY DODSON & RACHEL DODSON COVER WILL MURAI VARIANT COVER
CHRIS ROSA ASSOCIATE EDITOR BRITTANY HOLZHERR EDITOR
MIKE COTTON SENIOR EDITOR
WONDER WOMAN CREATED BY WILLIAM MOULTON MARSTON

ICELAND, LATER.
--THE EMERGENCY LANDING WAS CONDUCTED SUCCESSFULLY WITH MINIMAL INJURIES SUSTAINED, BUT FOR MANY THE QUESTION STILL REMAINS...

...WHAT EXACTLY COMPROMISED THE AIRCRAFT'S DOOR?
CONSPIRACY THEORIES ARE POURING IN, EVERYTHING FROM ***TERRORISM*** TO ***ALIENS.*** BUT AT THIS TIME, THE DETAILS REMAIN UNKNOWN.

EVEN MORE PERPLEXINGLY, AFTER QUESTIONING FROM THE ICELANDIC TRANSPORT AUTHORITY IT APPEARS THAT NONE OF THE AIR CREW OR PASSENGERS CAN REMEMBER THE EVENTS THAT TRANSPIRED ON FLIGHT 623.

I CAN'T BELIEVE THAT ACTUALLY WORKED. YOU REALLY MADE EVERYONE FORGET WHAT THEY SAW?
YEAH...BUT IT WASN'T EASY.
TAMPERING WITH THOUGHTS, MIND CONTROL...IT'S A SLIPPERY SLOPE. I DON'T LIKE DOING IT TO ONE PERSON, LET ALONE A WHOLE PLANE FULL.
BUT SOMETIMES YOU GOTTA ERASE A FEW MEMORIES WHEN YOU'RE TRYING TO KEEP A LOW PROFILE.
SKÅL!

MIND CONTROL... COULD IT BE HIM? A NEW MANIFESTATION OF HIS ABILITIES?
I SAW HIM RECENTLY, AND HE'S JUST AS ANGRY AS HE WAS IN ASGARD...
WHO, DR. PSYCHO?

HE'S GOING BY CIZKO NOW.
WHAT, IS HE REBRANDING NOW THAT HE'S TRYING TO TAKE HIS HALF-BAKED MESSAGE TO THE MAINSTREAM?

THAT ABOUT SUMS IT UP. THE WORST PART IS, PEOPLE ARE BUYING INTO IT.
HIS BOOK IS A BESTSELLER. SINCE I'VE BEEN BACK I CAN'T TURN ON THE TV WITHOUT HIM BEING ON IT, PREACHING HIS POISONOUS IDEOLOGY.

THESE ARE UNCERTAIN TIMES. PEOPLE ARE SCARED, AND CIZKO CAN SMELL IT.
HE SEES PEOPLE LOOKING FOR SAFETY, AND SWOOPS DOWN WITH ANSWERS THEY WANT TO HEAR.
IT'S PREDATORY.

THAT'S EXACTLY WHAT MAKES ME THINK HE'S INVOLVED.
I NEED TO FIGURE OUT WHERE THOSE THINGS CAME FROM.

WE. I'M IN THIS TOO. DO YOU WANT TO POSTPONE THIS SWORD THING? I MEAN, SWEDEN ISN'T GOING ANYWHERE.
NOT THAT I'M AWARE OF, BUT I'VE BEEN WRONG BEFORE.

NO. I'D LIKE TO FINISH WHAT WE STARTED.
THOSE THINGS FOUND US ON A PLANE--IT'S SAFE TO ASSUME THEY'LL LOCATE US AGAIN JUST AS EASILY. IN WHICH CASE, BEING IN THE MIDDLE OF NOWHERE WILL HAVE ITS BENEFITS.

MY MOTHER WANTS ME TO RETURN TO THEMYSCIRA SOON, BUT I CAN'T RISK LEADING THOSE THINGS TO THE ISLAND.
IT SEEMS LIKE TENSIONS ARE HIGH EVERYWHERE.

AND I STILL HAVEN'T TALKED TO STEVE YET! AGH.
YOU'LL GET NO JUDGMENT FROM ME. I KNOW WHAT YOU HAD TO GO THROUGH JUST TO BE HERE RIGHT NOW.
I WON'T SAY DON'T WORRY, BUT WE WILL SORT IT ALL OUT. NOW LET'S TRY AND GET SOME SHUT-EYE.
SIGH... YOU'RE RIGHT. BREAKFAST TOMORROW?

SURE. I'VE ALWAYS WONDERED WHAT THEY HAVE FOR BREKKIE IN ICELAND!
I'M AFRAID YOU'LL HAVE TO KEEP WONDERING--TOMORROW WE DINE IN UPPSALA.
CLIK

OOOH, A SWEDISH BREAKFAST! FANCY. I CAN'T WAIT.
GO TO SLEEP, BOSTON.

SWEDEN, 8:15 A.M.
...THEN HE LOOKED STRAIGHT AT ME AND SAID, DEAD SERIOUS, "WELL, AS TWO HONORABLE MEN..."
HAH! SIGGY IS SUCH A GOOD DUDE. I WISH I GOT TO HANG OUT WITH HIM MORE. HE SEEMED LIKE A LOT OF FUN.
OH, HE WAS. THERE WAS THIS ONE TIME--
BEEP
BEEP

GODS-- HE LEFT ME A VOICE MAIL.
SIEGFRIED?!
NO! HIM-- STEVE.

STEVE?
ETTA MUST HAVE GIVEN HIM MY NEW NUMBER. I DON'T KNOW WHY I NEVER GOT THE CALL--MAYBE IT WAS WHILE WE WERE FLYING. I... SIGH
I HAVE TO CALL HIM BACK.
YOU GOT THIS.
THANK YOU. I WON'T BE LONG.
AND IN THE MEANTIME, I SHALL TRY NOT TO EAT ALL OF THESE CUTE LITTLE SANDWICHES...

WASHINGTON, D.C., 2:19 A.M.
RIIIING

DIANA?
IT'S THE MIDDLE OF THE NIGHT. I...ARE YOU OKAY?
HELLO?

YOU'RE BREAKING UP PRETTY BAD. I CAN'T UNDERSTAND WHAT YOU'RE SAYING--
WHERE ARE YOU?

SWEDEN? WHAT ARE YOU--
HELLO?
DIANA?
DIANA...!
Call Disconnected

LIVE, FROM AN UNDISCLOSED LOCATION.
A DISCONNECT.
THAT'S ALL IT IS--IT'S LIKE MAKING AN INTERNATIONAL CALL ON A CHEAP CELL PHONE.

BUT THERE ARE THOSE AMONG US WHO POSSESS A STRONGER CONNECTION, AS I EXPLAIN IN MY BESTSELLING BOOK, *THE DELUSION.*
THERE ARE WAYS TO TAP INTO THE OTHER PLANES OF EXISTENCE, AND IT'S EASIER THAN YOU MIGHT THINK.
UNLIMITED NIGHTS AND WEEKENDS.
HA HA HA!

BEHOLD, AS I CALL FORTH THE GODFATHER OF MODERN ATHEISM--A ***NONBELIEVER*** IN LIFE, YET HIS SPIRIT IS STILL BOUND TO THE VERY TRUTHS THAT MY BOOK REVEALS!
MATTHIAS KNUTZEN!

SPEAKETH, O FATHER OF DISBELIEF!
SPEAKETH THROUGH ***ME,*** DR. EDGAR CIZKO!

GAH!

YES...IT IS I, CALLED FORTH FROM THE GREAT AND MYSTERIOUS BEYOND.
I BRING GOOD NEWS!
OOOOOHHH!
CLAPCLAPCLAP

I SPENT MY LIFE DENYING THE TRUTH--A TRUTH THAT I WILL SHARE WITH YOU TONIGHT!
MY FRIENDS--DEATH IS NOT THE END!
CLAP CLAP CLAP

LISTEN TO DR. CIZKO--HE WILL NOT LEAD YOU ASTRAAAAAY--
CLAP CLAP CLAP
HURK! STOP, WAIT--WAIT!

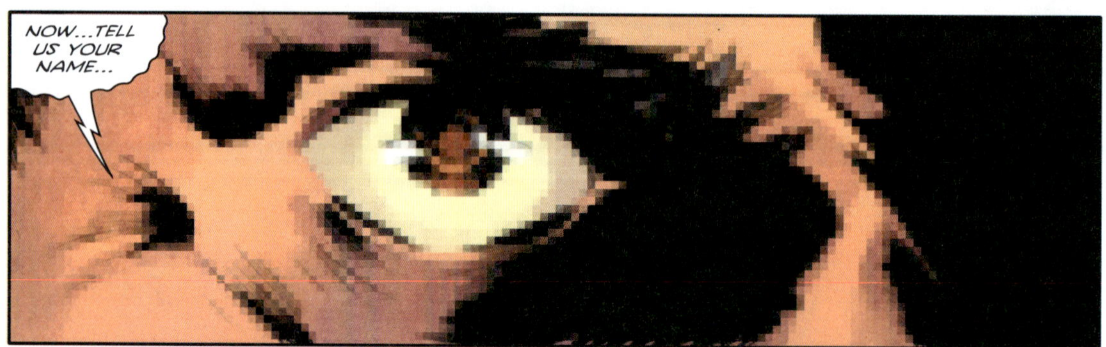

TUNE IN NEXT WEEK AS DR. CIZKO REVEALS THE SECRETS THEY DON'T WANT YOU TO KNOW!
BEE-BEE-BEE BOOP
BEE-BEE-BEE BOOP
Dr. Cizko's UNDOING DELUSION

I TOLD HIM NOT TO BE CALLING SO LATE...
WE MAY BE PARTNERS, BUT STILL--IT'S UN-PROFESSIONAL.
STEVE? WHAT GIVES--
THANK GOD YOU'RE UP! QUICK, PUT ON CHANNEL TWELVE.
Dr. Cizko's UNDOING DELUSION

MY GOD... WHAT AM I LOOKING AT?
THAT'S WHAT YOU'RE GOING TO HELP FIND OUT.
--FOOTAGE RECOVERED FROM A PASSENGER ABOARD FLIGHT 623'S CELL PHONE SUGGESTS THAT THE UNEXPLAINED INCIDENT WAS CAUSED BY MULTIPLE WONDER WOMEN--
BREAKING NEWS
WONDER WOMEN ATTACK FLIGHT 623?

CANCEL ALL ASSIGNMENTS--THIS IS OUR NEW PRIORITY.
WE WANNA KNOW WHAT THESE THINGS ARE, WHERE THEY COME FROM, AND HOW WE STOP THEM.

I HAD ONE PAY ME A PERSONAL VISIT.
WE NEED TO CONTAIN THESE THINGS.
COPY THAT.
I'M ALL OVER IT, COLONEL TREVOR.

I KNOW I CAN COUNT ON YOU.
LIKE TAXES. I'LL GET TO THE BOTTOM OF IT.

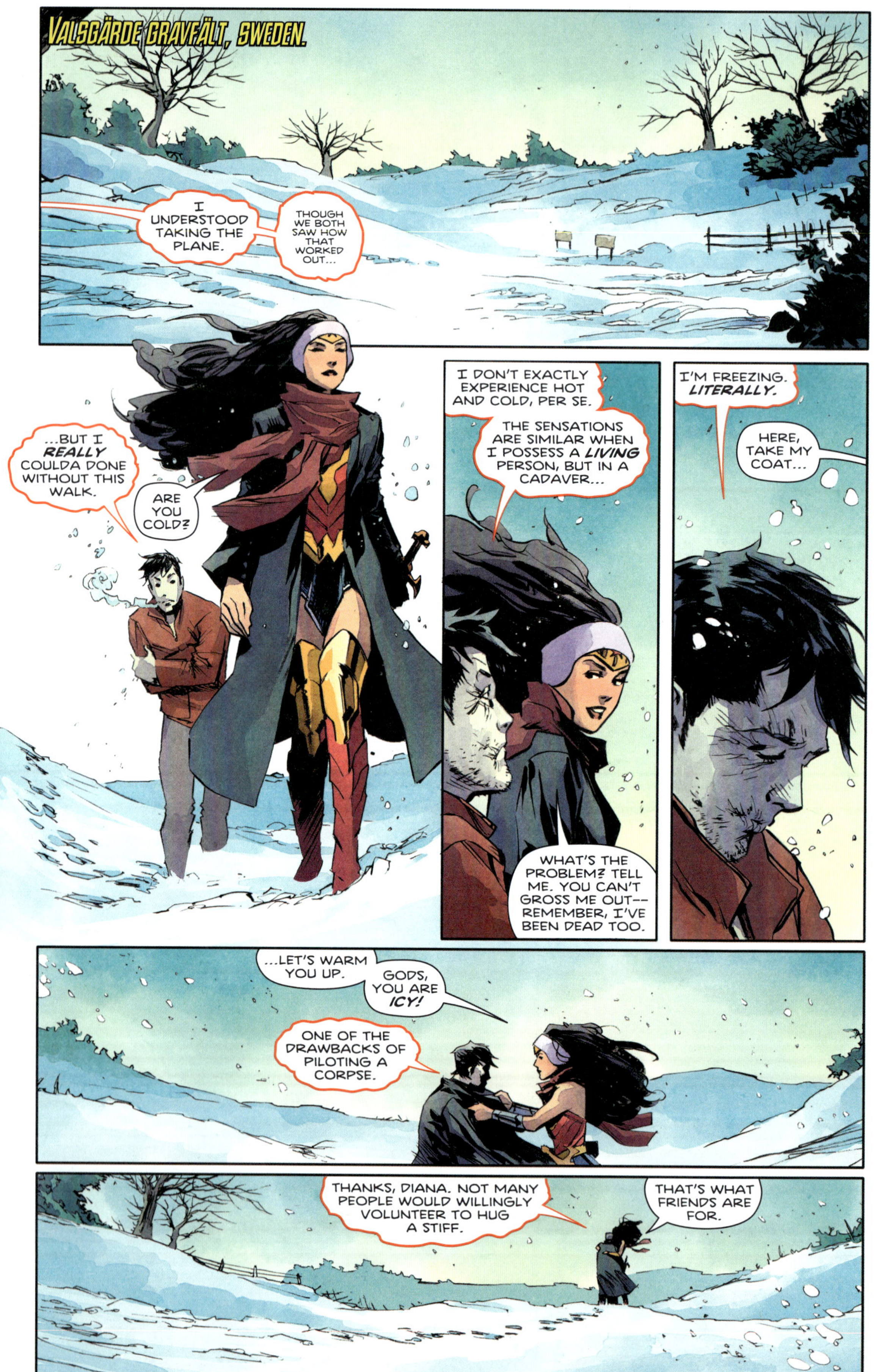
VALSGÄRDE GRAVFÄLT, SWEDEN.
I UNDERSTOOD TAKING THE PLANE.
THOUGH WE BOTH SAW HOW THAT WORKED OUT...
...BUT I REALLY COULDA DONE WITHOUT THIS WALK.
ARE YOU COLD?
I DON'T EXACTLY EXPERIENCE HOT AND COLD, PER SE.
THE SENSATIONS ARE SIMILAR WHEN I POSSESS A LIVING PERSON, BUT IN A CADAVER...
WHAT'S THE PROBLEM? TELL ME. YOU CAN'T GROSS ME OUT-- REMEMBER, I'VE BEEN DEAD TOO.
I'M FREEZING. LITERALLY.
HERE, TAKE MY COAT...
...LET'S WARM YOU UP.
GODS, YOU ARE ICY!
ONE OF THE DRAWBACKS OF PILOTING A CORPSE.
THANKS, DIANA. NOT MANY PEOPLE WOULD WILLINGLY VOLUNTEER TO HUG A STIFF.
THAT'S WHAT FRIENDS ARE FOR.

WE'RE PRETTY CLOSE NOW.
HOW CAN YOU TELL? WHAT DOES IT FEEL LIKE?

IT'S LIKE I'M SENSING A *RESONANCE*... VIBRATIONS.
HE MAY HAVE DIED LONG AGO, BUT SIEGFRIED WAS POWERFUL. HIS DEATH LEFT BEHIND A STRONG SIGNATURE.

WHAT OF PEOPLE WHO LIVE MORE ORDINARY LIVES? DO THEY JUST...FADE AWAY?

EVERY LIFE COUNTS, NO MATTER HOW BIG OR SMALL. YOU KNOW THIS, DIANA.
WHAT I FEEL HERE, THOUGH, IT'S *DIFFERENT.*

IN WHAT WAY?
SOME PEOPLE LEAVE BEHIND A TRACE OF THEMSELVES THAT FADES OVER TIME, LIKE AN ECHO. THOSE WHO ENCOUNTER ONE OFTEN MISTAKE IT FOR A GHOST.
IN THE CASE OF YOUR SIGGY, HOWEVER...

...IT'S A FEELING OF WORK LEFT TO BE DONE.
HIS DEATH WAS SUDDEN, UNEXPECTED. HE WASN'T FINISHED HERE.
THIS KIND OF LONGING...IT DOESN'T DIE WHEN YOU DO. I'M SORRY IF THIS ISN'T EASY TO HEAR.
...NO. BUT IT'S NICE TO KNOW MORE ABOUT HIM. EVEN IF IT'S DIFFICULT.

SO THIS IS IT. THE RUNESTONE MARKS HIS GRAVE?
...CAN YOU TELL ME HOW IT HAPPENED?
I CAN'T SAY FOR CERTAIN THAT IT'S HIS RESTING PLACE. PERHAPS IT WAS THE SITE OF HIS DEATH...IN ANY CASE, THIS IS WHERE THE VIBRATIONS EMANATE FROM.
THAT REMAINS MYSTERIOUS TO ME...BUT MAKE NO MISTAKE, HIS END WAS A *VIOLENT* ONE.
HE DIDN'T SEE IT COMING. IN A WAY THIS IS A BLESSING...IN MY EXPERIENCE, ANYHOW.
BUT HE HAD DREAMS LEFT UNFULFILLED. HE WISHED TO UNITE THE PEOPLE. TO END CONFLICTS THAT--
WELL...HE WAS A LOT LIKE *YOU,* DIANA.
I KNOW.

SCHLINK
THANK YOU, SIGGY. FOR YOUR FRIENDSHIP, YOUR BRAVERY. YOUR...
...EVERYTHING.
SHUNK
...FEEL BETTER?
MM. YEAH, I THINK I DO.
RIIING
YIKES. YOU DIDN'T SILENCE YOUR PHONE?!
I ALWAYS FORGET I EVEN HAVE ONE!

IT'S COOL, WE'RE FINISHED HERE. GO ON, TAKE IT.
THANK YOU. I'M--I MEAN, IT MIGHT BE IMPORTANT.

HELLO? STEVE?
YES...I CAN HEAR YOU. THERE'S SO MUCH I'VE WANTED TO SAY--
--OH... YOU SAW THAT? WAIT, WHAT?!
WHEN? HOW MANY?
NO, I UNDERSTAND. WE'LL BE RIGHT THERE.
STEVE... HELLO?
STEVE?
EVERYTHING KOSHER?
IT'S WORSE THAN WE THOUGHT.
WE'VE GOT TO GET BACK. NOW.

AT THAT EXACT MOMENT IN WASHINGTON, D.C.
WAIT, WHAT DO YOU MEAN, "WE"? WHO IS WE?
--DIANA?
FOR CRYIN' OUT LOUD...
WHAT THE HELL IS THAT? ALIENS?!
C'MON...
HEY! IS THE JUSTICE LEAGUE IN TOWN?
IT LOOKS LIKE...
...WONDER WOMAN!
LOTS OF WONDER WOMEN!
NO...
WE NEED MORE TIME!

SO THE DUPES ARE BACK?
THE WHAT?
DUPES.
YOU KNOW, DUPLICATES... OF YOU.
CUTE. HEY...ARE YOU GONNA BE ALL RIGHT? YOU LOOK A LITTLE, AH, MORE DECEASED THAN USUAL.

ME? I'LL BE GRAND. THIS BODY THOUGH--IT'S SEEN BETTER DAYS.
I USUALLY LIKE TO GIVE MY HOSTS A PROPER SEND-OFF, BUT WE MIGHT HAVE TO SETTLE FOR A BURIAL AT SEA.
YOU... WANT ME TO DROP YOU?
INTO THE ATLANTIC. YES. NOW.

WHOOSH

AH, THAT'S THE DEADMAN I'M USED TO! FEELING BETTER?
MUCH. NOW WHERE WERE WE?
OH YEAH, FIGURE OUT WHAT'S UP WITH THESE DUPES.
AS USUAL...

"...WE DON'T EXACTLY KNOW WHAT WE'RE UP AGAINST."
THAT'S RIGHT, WONDER WOMAN...
FOLLOW THE REFLECTIONS. LET YOUR OWN LIKENESS LEAD YOU TO YOUR ***RIGHTFUL DOMAIN.***
COME TO ME.

COME TO THE IMAGE-MAKER!...
...MASTER OF MIRROR-WORLD!

Wonder Woman #783
cover by TERRY DODSON
and RACHEL DODSON

***Wonder Woman* #783**
variant cover by WILL MURAI

WELCOME, MY NEW FRIEND. PLEASE, MAKE YOURSELF COMFORTABLE.
WHEN THEY SAID THEY'D SEND ME A CHAMPION, NEVER IN MY WILDEST DREAMS DID I THINK IT WOULD BE YOU!
I'M SURE YOU'RE WONDERING WHAT YOU ARE DOING HERE. WE'LL GET TO ALL THAT, I ASSURE YOU...
THE DELUSION
DR. EDGAR CIZKO'S TOWNHOUSE. WASHINGTON, D.C.
...BUT FIRST, ALLOW ME TO ANOINT YOU WITH A FEW GIFTS.
AS WE ALL KNOW, EVERY HONORABLE PALADIN NEEDS A PROPER SUIT OF ARMOR.
BOW TO ME AND PLACE THIS HELM UPON THINE HEAD.
VERY GOOD. AND NOW FOR THE FINISHING TOUCH...

YOU WILL FOLLOW MY ORDERS, AND MINE ALONE.

THIS, MY FRIEND--*THIS* WILL BE OUR MEANS OF SENDING THAT WENCH BACK TO THE AFTERLIFE!

YOU WILL BE MY AGENT, MY VASSAL, MY ARM WITH WHICH I SHALL CRUSH MY ENEMIES!

WHEN YOU STRIKE, IT WILL BE SWIFT AND WITHOUT MERCY.

WONDER WOMAN SOON WILL FALL TO MY MIGHT, AND YOU WILL BE MY CHEVALIER...

...MY SHINING KNIGHT!

Yes, m'lord.

THROUGH A GLASS DARKLY
PART THREE

MICHAEL W. CONRAD & BECKY CLOONAN WRITERS
MARCIO TAKARA ARTIST TAMRA BONVILLAIN COLORIST
PAT BROSSEAU LETTERER TERRY DODSON & RACHEL DODSON COVER WILL MURAI VARIANT COVER
CHRIS ROSA ASSOCIATE EDITOR BRITTANY HOLZHERR EDITOR
MIKE COTTON SENIOR EDITOR
WONDER WOMAN CREATED BY WILLIAM MOULTON MARSTON

WASHINGTON, D.C.
SWEET RAMA KUSHNA--
WHERE DO YOU THINK THEY'RE ALL COMING FROM?
DOWN THERE? BUT THE WAY IS BLOCKED...
LET'S GO, DEADMAN.
ETTA TELLS ME SHE AND STEVE HAVE STARTED WORKING WITH CHECKMATE.* IF ANYONE CAN GET A LEAD ON THIS, IT'S THEM.
*SEE CHECKMATE! --BRITTANY
I'LL CLEAR A PATH!
KRASH

WE ARE SHE.
WE ARE WONDER WOMAN.
HIT THEM HARD!
KRASH
YEAH? IS THAT THE MOVE?
I WAS WONDERING ABOUT THAT BIT...
SMASH
DO YOU NEED ANOTHER DEMONSTRATION?
KSSSHT

UNG-- THAT'S GREAT, BUT--
LIKE I SAID BEFORE, THEY-- HNGH! THERE'S TOO MANY!
KSSSH

CAN YOU HOLD THEM OFF? I'M GOING TO SEE IF ETTA HAS IDENTIFIED THEIR SOURCE.
I'LL TRY--

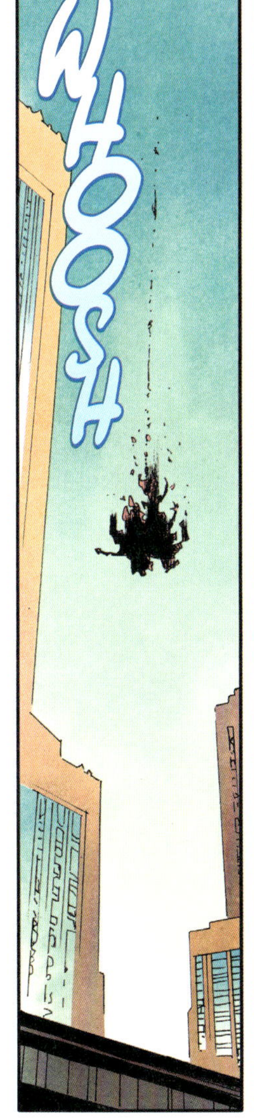
WHOOSH

KSSSH

HMM...

...A MIRROR?

ELSEWHERE.
WHEN YOU STARE INTO A LOOKING GLASS, DO YOU EVER WONDER ABOUT THE ONE WHO GAZES BACK?

IF YOU LOOK CLOSE ENOUGH, YOU'LL START TO SEE THE CRACKS...

...THE PERSON IN THE MIRROR IS REAL, AND IT IS *YOU* WHO IS THE REFLECTION.

COME, WONDER WOMAN. STARE INTO THE MIRROR.
LET YOUR OWN IMAGE LEAD YOU *HOME.*

"--I *KNOW* THEY JUST ATTACKED THE CAPITAL--
"I'M JUST SAYING, WITH THE ANGLE MY DRONE HAS ON THEM, THEY LOOK KINDA PRETTY.

"COPY THAT. I'M GOING TO SCRAMBLE A SQUAD OF F-35s--THAT SHOULD KEEP 'EM BUSY.

WHAT AM *I* DOING? I'M FOLLOWING THESE THINGS TO THEIR *SOURCE!* WHAT YOU YOU THINK I'M--
--OH!
IMPROMPTU CHECKMATE HEADQUARTERS. WASHINGTON, D.C.

STEVE, I NEED TO CALL YOU BACK.
STAY SAFE OUT THERE.
"I GOT YOU NOW, YOU SON OF A--"
HALL OF MIRRORS
TAFFY'S
DES AND GAMES
CLOSED UNTIL FURTHER NOTICE

HUMMEL STREET, D.C. FINANCIAL DISTRICT.
EVERYONE, GET TO COVER!
INSIDE! NOW!
BRAK BRAK BRAK

BRAK BRAK
C'MON, KID! YOU TOO.

EVERYTHING'S GONNA BE OKAY. YOU GOT PARENTS, RIGHT? LET'S GO FIND THEM.
IS THAT... WONDER WOMAN?

WELL, WOULD YA LOOK AT THAT?

IMPROMPTU CHECKMATE HEADQUARTERS, TWELFTH-FLOOR STAIRWELL.

~HUFF~
~HUFF~

C'MON, CANDY, MOVE IT! ~HUFF~

...NO DIFFERENT FROM THE DANG STAIR MACHINE. ~HUFF~ YOU GOT THIS!

...ALMOST THERE, PUSH! ~HUFF~

~HUFF~

~HUFF~

WHAM

WONDER WOMAN!
HEY, DOWN HERE!
I PINPOINTED THE SOURCE-- ~HUFF~ ~HUFF~
--FOUND WHERE THEY'RE COMING FROM!

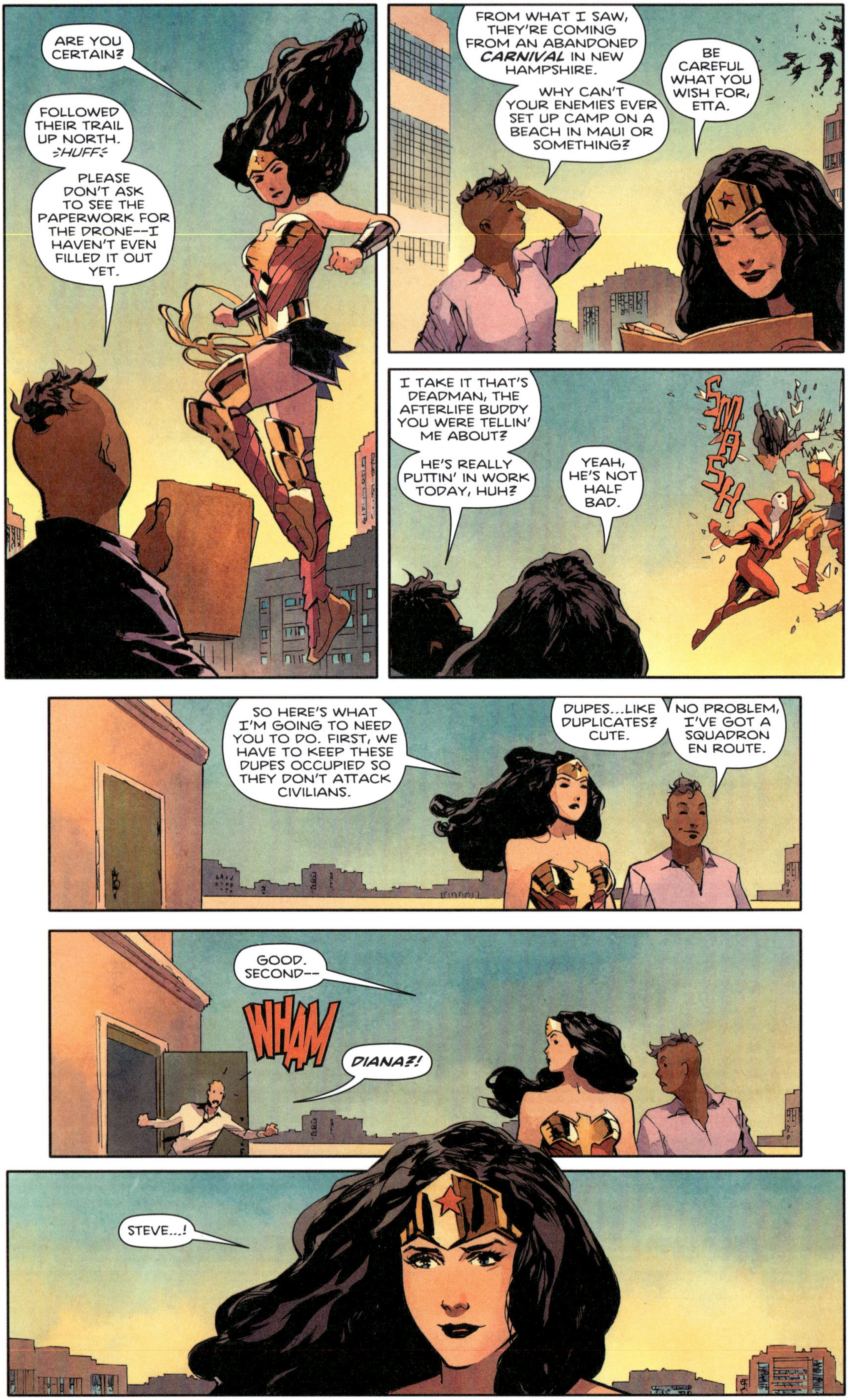

ARE YOU CERTAIN?
FOLLOWED THEIR TRAIL UP NORTH. *HUFF*
PLEASE DON'T ASK TO SEE THE PAPERWORK FOR THE DRONE--I HAVEN'T EVEN FILLED IT OUT YET.
FROM WHAT I SAW, THEY'RE COMING FROM AN ABANDONED **CARNIVAL** IN NEW HAMPSHIRE.
WHY CAN'T YOUR ENEMIES EVER SET UP CAMP ON A BEACH IN MAUI OR SOMETHING?
BE CAREFUL WHAT YOU WISH FOR, ETTA.
I TAKE IT THAT'S DEADMAN, THE AFTERLIFE BUDDY YOU WERE TELLIN' ME ABOUT?
HE'S REALLY PUTTIN' IN WORK TODAY, HUH?
YEAH, HE'S NOT HALF BAD.
SMASH

YOU MUST BE STEVE! HIYA, I'M BOSTON.

I DON'T BELIEVE WE'VE MET, BUT I'VE HEARD A *LOT* ABOUT YOU...

ONLY GOOD THINGS, RIGHT? HA HA!

DEADMAN, IF YOU DON'T STOP TALKING YOU'RE GOING TO LIVE UP TO YOUR NAME--

SHA-THOOM

--TYPHON'S MIGHT! EVERYBODY, ***DOWN!***

To your feet.
WHO DARES CHALLENGE DIANA OF THEMYSCIRA?
SPEAK NOW AND MAKE IT SWIFT. I HAVEN'T TIME FOR NONSENSE.
I am the Shining Knight...
...and you, m'lady, are my quest.
Now rise!
WHOOOOOSH
Meet my blade, and your final moments!

KLANG
SKISSH
I HAVE NO QUARREL WITH YOU. STEP ASIDE, THERE ARE PEOPLE IN DANGER!
M'lord has requested your head on a pike. I will not stand down until his demand has been met.
YOU WANT MY HEAD? I WELCOME YOU TO TRY AND TAKE IT--BUT AT LEAST HAVE THE COURTESY TO TELL ME WHO IT IS I FIGHT.
SURELY YOU ARE NOT SIR JUSTIN!
Who am I? Why, Wonder Woman...I am your reckoning!
KLANG

AS A KNIGHT, HAVE YOU NO CHIVALRIC CODE? I ASK YOU AGAIN--*WHO ARE YOU?*

*I am he who would serve the **archmage** of this confounding era!*

NO OFFENSE, BUT YOU TWO ARE OUT OF YOUR DEPTH UP HERE.
HE'S RIGHT. MOVE IT, ETTA! HEAD FOR THE STAIRS--
I KNOW WHERE I'M GOIN'. WE GOT DUPES TO WRANGLE!
At least your compatriots have sense enough to leave.
They must not wish to see you slain by my hand.
I'D SAY YOUR WORDS ARE MORE EFFECTIVE THAN YOUR SWORD...
WHOOOOOSH
WHACK
...BUT HONESTLY? NEITHER HAS TRULY IMPRESSED ME!

It will matter not when I cleave your skull in twain!

WIFF

BOSTON, WHO IS THIS IMPOSTOR?

I CAN'T... ***HNNGH!*** I CAN'T REACH HIM!

SWIPP

WHAT DO YOU MEAN?

I CAN'T GET IN HIS HEAD! I DON'T KNOW IF IT'S HIS HELMET OR WHAT, BUT--

COME, KNIGHT.
YOU WANT A FIGHT? LET IT BE A FIGHT, THEN.

That's the spirit, old hag!
Give us a challenge!
GREAT GODDESS-- YOU CAN FLY!

NOW LET'S SEE IF YOU CAN CATCH.

WHISH
SCHWACK
NOW I'M JUST SHOWING OFF.
THMP
You dare toy with me?

WHEN I'M THROUGH WITH YOU, I WILL RIP THAT RIDICULOUS HELM FROM YOUR HEAD!

I WILL KNOW WHO YOU ARE, AND I WILL FORGET YOU IN THE SAME BREATH.

THEN, WHEN YOU CRAWL BROKEN AND BLOODY BACK TO ***CIZKO,*** KINDLY TELL THE ***GOOD DOCTOR*** THAT I'M COMING FOR HIM.

FWOOSH

How?! What witchery is this?

WITCHERY? ONE HARDLY NEEDS ***MAGIC*** TO KNOW WHAT MASTER YOU TRULY SERVE...

--HOLA!

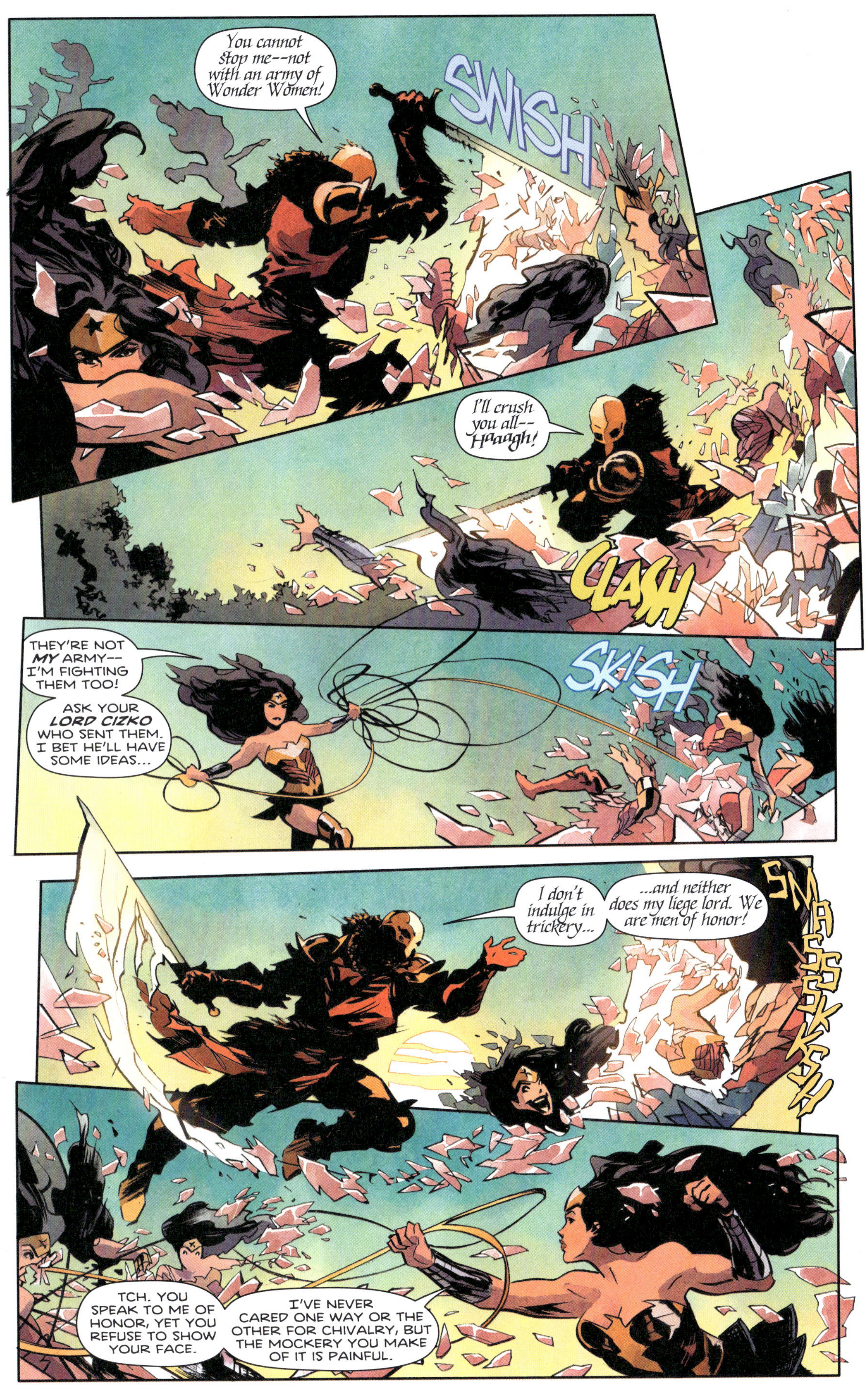
You cannot stop me--not with an army of Wonder Women!
SWISH
I'll crush you all-- Haaagh!
CLASH
THEY'RE NOT MY ARMY-- I'M FIGHTING THEM TOO!
ASK YOUR LORD CIZKO WHO SENT THEM. I BET HE'LL HAVE SOME IDEAS...
SKISH
I don't indulge in trickery...
...and neither does my liege lord. We are men of honor!
SMASSSKSH
TCH. YOU SPEAK TO ME OF HONOR, YET YOU REFUSE TO SHOW YOUR FACE.
I'VE NEVER CARED ONE WAY OR THE OTHER FOR CHIVALRY, BUT THE MOCKERY YOU MAKE OF IT IS PAINFUL.

Then for you, I shall renew my chivalric vows!
I swear I will see these look-alikes defeated before I raise my sword to you again, m'lady.
VERY GOOD...
...BUT PLEASE, NEVER CALL ME M'LADY AGAIN.
Have at thee! Haagh!
SMASH
KLASH
CRASH

MEANWHILE IN THEMYSCIRA...
MY DAUGHTER, CAN YOU HEAR ME?
*THIS TAKES PLACE AFTER THE EVENTS OF NUBIA & THE AMAZONS #5. -- BRITTANY
DIANA... I'VE BEEN TRYING TO CONTACT YOU FOR DAYS.
YOU ARE NEEDED HERE--AT HOME.
YES...
...I AM SHE.
I AM WONDER WOMAN.
YOU ARE NOT!

WE ARE WONDER WOMAN.
WE WILL FIND HER. WE WILL LEAD HER TO HER TRUE HOME.
WE WILL KILL THOSE IN OUR WAY.

YOU WOULD KILL ME?!

HA!
CRASH

I SHALL NEVER DIE.

Wonder Woman #784
cover by TERRY DODSON
and RACHEL DODSON

***Wonder Woman* #784**
variant cover by WILL MURAI

TWO HUNDRED AND THIRTY FEET ABOVE TAFFY'S RIDES AND GAMES. HAMPTON BEACH, NH.
BELOW US-- LOOK! THAT MUST BE THE ABANDONED CARNIVAL. SUFFERING SAPPHO, ETTA WAS RIGHT. THIS DOES SEEM TO BE THE SOURCE OF THESE DUPES.
I HOPE YOU'RE PREPARED TO BRING THE FIGHT!
Fear not, Woman of Wonder. I remain true to my vow!
I shall vanquish these doubles, with strength enough remaining to finish our duel-- and finish you!
SMASH
THROUGH A GLASS DARKLY
FINALE
MICHAEL W. CONRAD & BECKY CLOONAN WRITERS MARCIO TAKARA ARTIST TAMRA BONVILLAIN COLORIST PAT BROSSEAU LETTERER TERRY DODSON & RACHEL DODSON COVER WILL MURAI VARIANT COVER CHRIS ROSA ASSOCIATE EDITOR BRITTANY HOLZHERR EDITOR PAUL KAMINSKI SENIOR EDITOR WONDER WOMAN CREATED BY WILLIAM MOULTON MARSTON

Behold! I know neither fear nor cowardice.

WHOOOSH

Haaah!

SSSKASSH

I have your word that you will not flee?

WHUMP

WELCOME, DIANA.
A HALL OF MIRRORS, HOW APPROPRIATE.
KRREE
WELCOME.
WELCOME. WE'VE BEEN WAITING.
WAITING FOR YOU.
FOR YOU.
KRASH
WHO'S BEHIND THIS SIDESHOW? SHOW YOURSELF!
YOU'RE PROBABLY JUST ANOTHER FAILED HERO IN YOUR OWN MIND, TOO SELF-RIGHTEOUS TO REALIZE YOU'VE BECOME THE VILLAIN.
CRASH
OH, DIANA. I HAVE NO DOUBTS ABOUT MY PERCEIVED VILLAINY IN THIS REALM.
I HAVE NOT COME HERE TO REDEEM MYSELF.

I AM THE *IMAGE-MAKER,* MASTER AND COMMANDER OF *MIRROR-WORLD.*
I HAVE COME TO THIS PALLID REALM TO TAKE YOU *HOME.*

I *AM* HOME!
CRASH

ARE YOU THOUGH? YOU *DIED,* DIANA. REBORN THROUGH SHEER FORCE OF WILL.
STILL, SOMETHING FEELS... *DIFFERENT.* YOU CAN'T EXACTLY PUT YOUR FINGER ON IT, BUT YOU CAN TELL SOMETHING'S CHANGED.
YOU'RE NOT THE SAME. *WHY?*
I SUPPOSE YOU HAVE SOME INSIGHT YOU'RE GOING TO SHARE WITH ME?

I *DO.*
YOU'RE A *REFLECTION.* A COPY OF THE PERSON YOU USED TO BE.

NONSENSE.
AHH, BUT THE PROOF IS RIGHT IN FRONT OF YOU.
MIRROR-WORLD, SO OFTEN OVERLOOKED, INVISIBLE TO OUTSIDERS--IT WAS *BROKEN* IN YOUR DESPERATE BID TO RETURN.
AND YOU, MY PRINCESS... YOU FELL THROUGH THE CRACKS.

I DID NO SUCH THING. I KNOW WHO I AM.
AHH, SO THINK WE ALL...
...BUT WE NEVER TRULY KNOW WHICH SIDE OF THE MIRROR IS THE REFLECTION.
I'VE HAD ENOUGH OF YOUR HEAD GAMES.
ON THE CONTRARY-- I ONLY SPEAK THE TRUTH. YOU LIKE THE TRUTH, DON'T YOU?
YOU CAME BACK TO A WORLD THAT DOESN'T NEED YOU ANYMORE. YOUR ROLE HAS BEEN FILLED BY OTHERS JUST AS CAPABLE.
THIS IS ABSURD.
IF YOU DON'T RETURN TO YOUR OWN REALM, I'LL CRUSH YOU LIKE ONE OF YOUR GLASS DUPES!
YOUR ANGER BETRAYS THE VERY DOUBT YOU FEEL!
OH YES, DIANA. I WILL RETURN--AND I'M TAKING YOU WITH ME.
NO!
FOR NOW YOU SEE THROUGH A GLASS, DARKLY...
LET ME OUT!
LOOK, DIANA!
SEE WHAT YOU HAVE FORSAKEN!

WHERE AM I?

WHAT'S GOING ON HERE?
DIANA?
HALL OF MIRRORS

DIANA! THANK GOODNESS, THERE YOU ARE!

STEVE?
I TURNED MY BACK AND YOU WANDERED OFF! FOR A MINUTE THERE I THOUGHT I'D LOST YOU.

WHAT HAPPENED TO THE *DUPES* WE WERE FIGHTING? AND THAT STRANGE *KNIGHT...?*
AND THIS DRESS... WHERE IS MY *COSTUME?*

DID YOU BUMP YOUR HEAD IN THE HALL OF MIRRORS?
I...
COME ON, YOU HAVEN'T BEEN WONDER WOMAN FOR AGES. YOU QUIT WHEN THERE WAS NO ONE LEFT TO FIGHT, REMEMBER?

IT'S JUST US NOW, AS IT WAS ALWAYS MEANT TO BE.

JUST US, HUH?
IT'S BEEN A LONG TIME SINCE WE'VE SHARED A MOMENT LIKE THIS.

IT FEELS SO NICE...

...BUT IT ISN'T REAL.

AS MUCH AS I WANT IT TO BE.
I'M SORRY, STEVE.

D-- DIANA?
KLASH

WITH YOU BY MY SIDE, OUR MIGHT WILL BE UNQUESTIONABLE!
WE WILL RESTORE THE REALM OF REFLECTIONS TO WHAT IT ALWAYS WAS...
...THE ONE TRUE REALITY, RATHER THAN A DIM REFLECTION OF *LESSERS!*
THIS IS THE TRUTH.
ITS SHINING LIGHT ALLOWS ME TO SEE THROUGH YOUR DECEPTION!
ALL PERCEPTION IS BUT AN ILLUSION FROM ANOTHER ANGLE.
I AM AT PEACE WITH THAT.
SHA KLASH

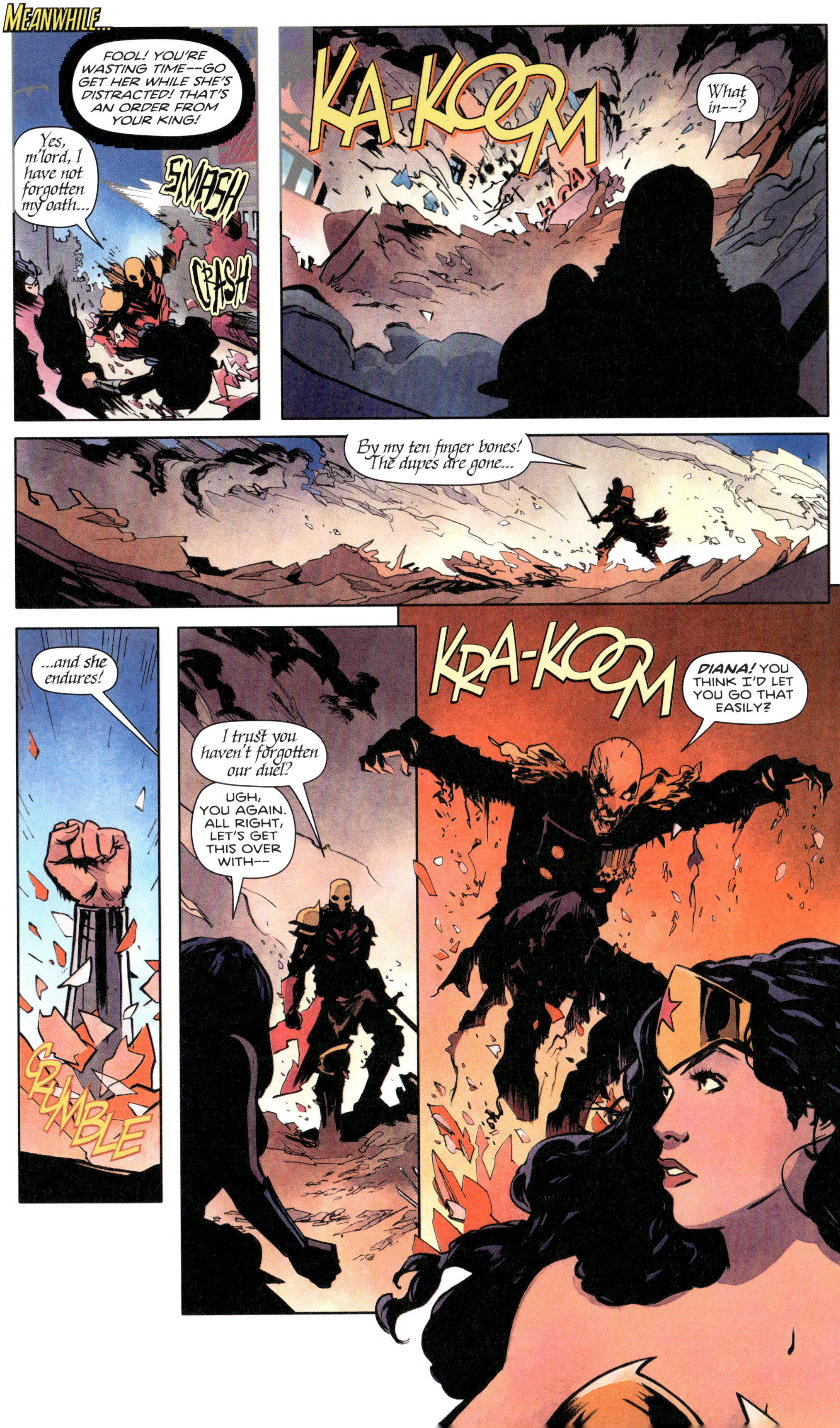

MEANWHILE...

FOOL! YOU'RE WASTING TIME--GO GET HER WHILE SHE'S DISTRACTED! THAT'S AN ORDER FROM YOUR KING!
Yes, m'lord, I have not forgotten my oath...
SMASH
CRASH

KA-KOOM
What in--?

By my ten finger bones! The dupes are gone...

...and she endures!
CRUMBLE

I trust you haven't forgotten our duel?

UGH, YOU AGAIN. ALL RIGHT, LET'S GET THIS OVER WITH--

KRA-KOOM

DIANA! YOU THINK I'D LET YOU GO THAT EASILY?

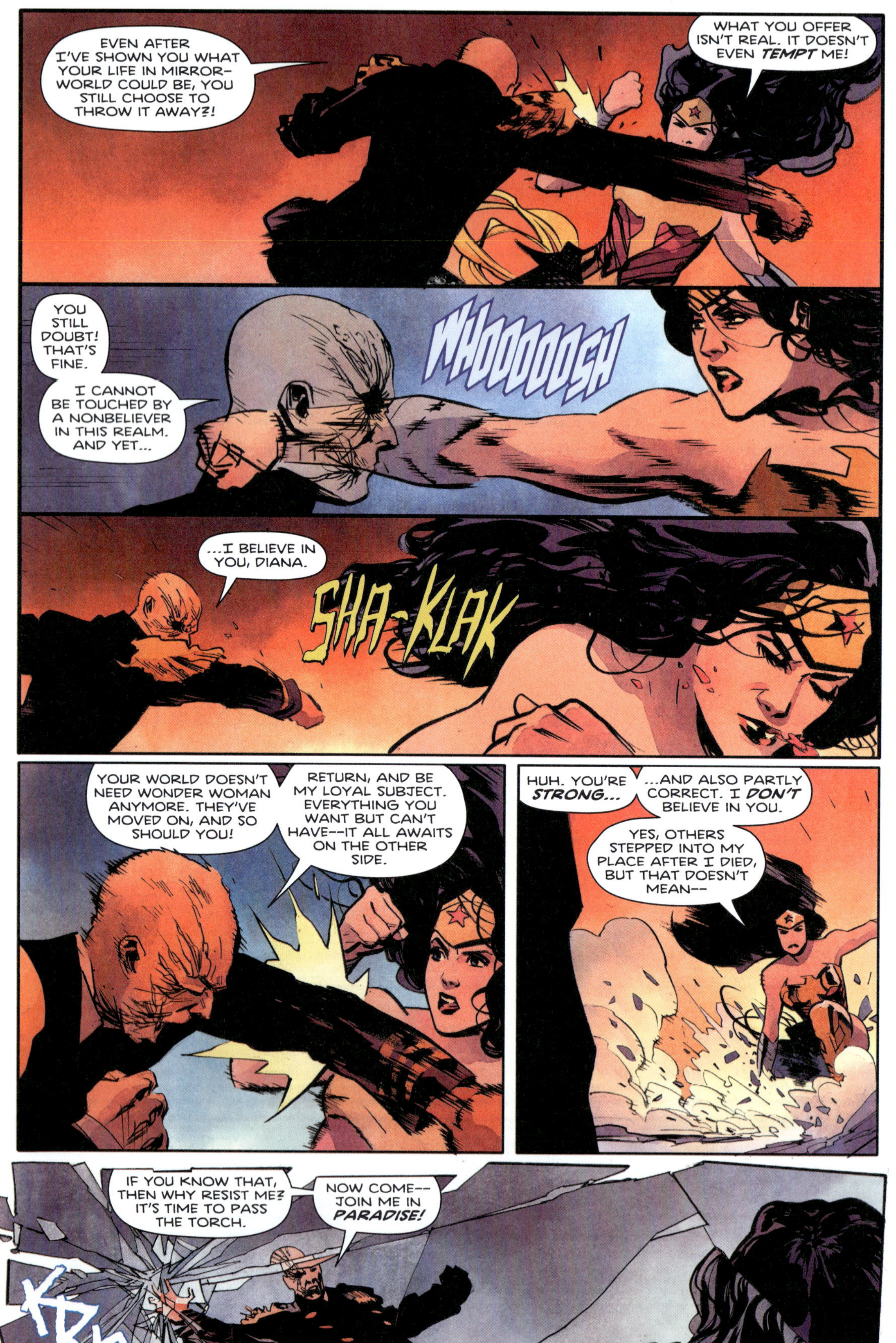

EVEN AFTER I'VE SHOWN YOU WHAT YOUR LIFE IN MIRROR-WORLD COULD BE, YOU STILL CHOOSE TO THROW IT AWAY?!
WHAT YOU OFFER ISN'T REAL. IT DOESN'T EVEN *TEMPT* ME!
YOU STILL DOUBT! THAT'S FINE.
I CANNOT BE TOUCHED BY A NONBELIEVER IN THIS REALM. AND YET...
WHOOOOOSH
...I BELIEVE IN YOU, DIANA.
SHA-KLAK
YOUR WORLD DOESN'T NEED WONDER WOMAN ANYMORE. THEY'VE MOVED ON, AND SO SHOULD YOU!
RETURN, AND BE MY LOYAL SUBJECT. EVERYTHING YOU WANT BUT CAN'T HAVE--IT ALL AWAITS ON THE OTHER SIDE.
HUH. YOU'RE *STRONG...*
...AND ALSO PARTLY CORRECT. I *DON'T* BELIEVE IN YOU.
YES, OTHERS STEPPED INTO MY PLACE AFTER I DIED, BUT THAT DOESN'T MEAN--
IF YOU KNOW THAT, THEN WHY RESIST ME? IT'S TIME TO PASS THE TORCH.
NOW COME-- JOIN ME IN *PARADISE!*
KRISH
DIANA!

HEADS UP!
GRAM...
NO!
SMASH
I MAY NOT BELIEVE, BUT THIS BLADE HAS SEEN YOU FOR WHAT YOU TRULY ARE--
--A MIRROR *CRACKED* FROM SIDE TO SIDE.
SHACASH
LEAVE NOW, AND *NEVER* RETURN!
LEAVE IT TO THE MASTER OF MIRROR-WORLD TO GET EVERYTHING *BACKWARD.*
SO, IS HE...
DEAD? I DON'T THINK SO, NO. WITHOUT FORM HE'S BEEN FORCED TO RETURN TO THE MIRROR-WORLD.
I DON'T WANT TO THINK THERE WAS TRUTH IN ANY OF THE THINGS HE SAID, BUT--
I see you've armed yourself...

...just in time to face me!
WHOA!
THIS GUY FOLLOWED YOU ALL THE WAY UP TO THE GRANITE STATE?
KLANG

HE'S PERSISTENT, I'LL GIVE HIM THAT MUCH.
YEAH. HE'S ABOUT TO BE *NONEXISTENT* TOO.
TOO BAD. HE'S GOT A COOL LOOK.

SO TELL ME, KNIGHT. SHOULD WE ESTABLISH SOME CODE OF CONDUCT?

No code. We fight to the death.

...AND WHAT SHALL I DO WITH YOUR BODY?
When we are finished...

...my body shall return to the earth!

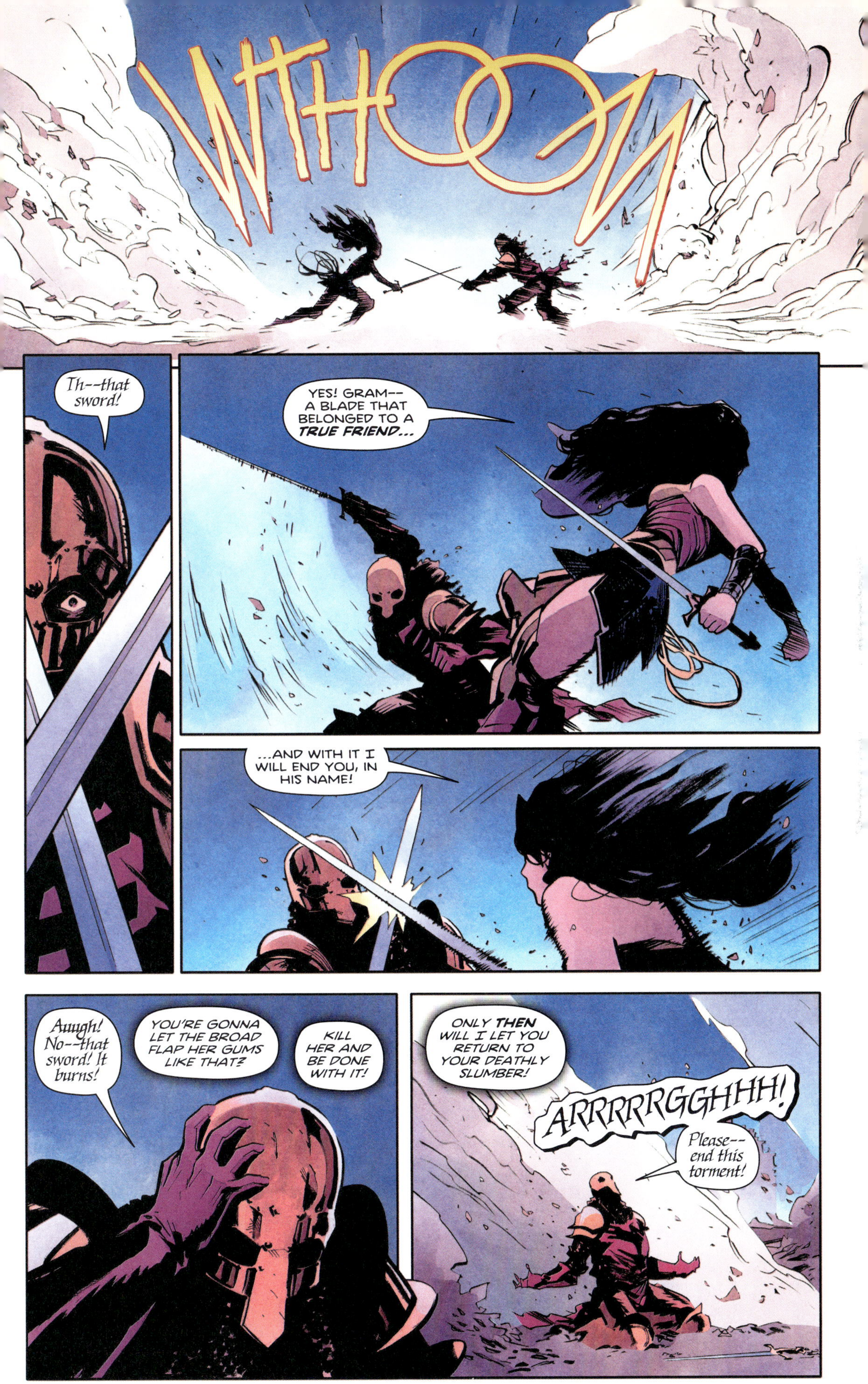

WHOOM

Th--that sword!

YES! GRAM-- A BLADE THAT BELONGED TO A **TRUE FRIEND...**

...AND WITH IT I WILL END YOU, IN HIS NAME!

Augh! No--that sword! It burns!
YOU'RE GONNA LET THE BROAD FLAP HER GUMS LIKE THAT?
KILL HER AND BE DONE WITH IT!
ONLY **THEN** WILL I LET YOU RETURN TO YOUR DEATHLY SLUMBER!
ARRRRRGGHHH!
Please-- end this torment!

TELL US WHO IS UNDER THIS MASK!
SNAP
I-- I don't know.

IF YOU'LL ALLOW ME--I'LL TRY AND FORCE WHOEVER IS CONTROLLING HIM OUT!
Aaaagh!
HE WAS SUPPOSED TO BE THIS GREAT CHAMPION!
TURNS OUT HE'S A SUCKER, JUST LIKE THE REST OF 'EM!

NO MATTER. THIS WAS A FUN GAME WHILE IT LASTED.
CIZKO! I KNOW YOU'RE THERE.

SHOW YOURSELF, COWARD!
IT'S NO USE, DIANA-- HE'S GONE. BUT YOUR KNIGHT... HIS MIND IS HIS OWN AGAIN.

I THINK...
...MAYBE I SHOULD LEAVE THIS NEXT BIT TO YOU.

I CAN FORGIVE YOU, KNIGHT--SEEING AS HOW YOU WERE ONLY ACTING UNDER CIZKO'S INFLUENCE.
BUT THE MYSTERY STILL REMAINS...
...DIANA?

I HEARD YOUR VOICE CALLING ME...

GREAT PAN'S PIPES!
I'M SORRY...

...MY MIND WAS NOT MY OWN.
I TRIED TO FIGHT, BUT I WASN'T STRONG ENOUGH...
SSH.

IT'S ALL RIGHT, *SIEGFRIED.*
I ALWAYS KNEW...YOU WOULD FIND ME IN THE FOG.

UNGH...
EASY, LET ME HELP YOU.

HOW DID YOU GET HERE? WAS IT...
WAS IT CIZKO? THE MAN CONTROLLING YOU?
I DON'T...

HIS WORKINGS... IT WAS DARK MAGIC. THE SERPENT...THE CHASM...
...THE APEIRON.

IS HE...?
TRAUMATIZED.
HE'S NOT *LIKE* YOU, DIANA. FEW CAN JUMP REALITIES WITHOUT IT TAKING A SERIOUS TOLL.
IF YOU HADN'T GONE BACK FOR HIS SWORD, I MIGHT HAVE...GODS, I WOULD HAVE *KILLED* HIM--

SSH. TAKE A MOMENT, GET SOME REST.
I'LL TAKE CARE OF SIGGY. YOU TAKE CARE OF *YOU.*
NO, YOU'RE RIGHT.
THANK YOU. I'LL CHECK IN SOON.

THE FOLLOWING DAY, WASHINGTON, D.C.
LORD, MY BACK IS SINGING.
SAME.
THANKS FOR JOINING THE CLEANUP CREW, ETTA. YOUR HELP MEANS A LOT.

HELPING YOU, AGENT TREVOR?
I MEAN, I APPRECIATE THAT YOU BOUGHT EVERYONE SMOOTHIES, BUT I'VE BEEN OUT HERE ALL DAY!

AND MY REPORT WILL CLEARLY REFLECT THAT HITTING THE JUICE BAR WAS A CRITICAL PART OF THE MISSION.
AND, UH, DINNER TOO. FOR TEAM MORALE.

NOW YOU'RE TALKING.
BISTRO VONISH?

PERFECT. GIMME AN HOUR TO CLEAN UP.
I DUNNO WHY THESE VESTS HAVE TO BE ORANGE. I LOOK AWFUL IN ORANGE.

HEY, JUST CHECKING-- YOU COOL? I KNOW A LOT'S HAPPENED.

YEAH...
YEAH. I THINK I'M GOOD.

SAINT ANTHONY HOSPITAL, BETHESDA, MD.
BEEP BEEP BEEP
IS THIS... MUSIC?
THAT'S YOUR *HEART,* SIGGY.
ACTUALLY, IT BEEPS WHEN YOUR HEART *ISN'T* BEATING. THE SOUND YOU HEAR IS THE PAUSE IN THE ACTION.
I HAVE LAIN SO LONG IN THE BURIAL MOUND...I'D FORGOTTEN WHAT IT FELT LIKE.

YOU'LL GET USED TO IT BEFORE TOO LONG. PERHAPS SOONER...WITH *YOUR BLADE* AT YOUR SIDE.
GRAM--! OH, DIANA. YOU KEPT YOUR WORD...
ALWAYS. I KNOW IT WAS A ROUGH JOURNEY. I'M GLAD I GOT TO SEE YOU BEFORE I DEPART.

YOU'RE LEAVING, SO SOON?
THERE ARE A FEW THINGS I MUST ATTEND TO...
NEVER YOU FEAR, SIEGFRIED! YOU'LL BE IN GOOD HANDS UNTIL SHE COMES BACK.
THE NURSE TOLD ME KEEPING YOU HERE IS A FORMALITY. THEY COULDN'T EVEN ATTACH AN I.V.--KEPT BREAKING NEEDLES ON YOUR SKIN.

A NEEDLE? DID I NEED... STITCHING?

I SEE I'VE GOT MY WORK CUT OUT FOR ME.
GO EASY ON HIM, BOSTON. SIGGY IS NEW HERE...
...HE'S GOT SOME CATCHING UP TO DO.

SAFE TRAVELS, DIANA.
I'LL COME BACK FOR YOU.

THEMYSCIRA.

WE'RE FINE, IT'S JUST BROKEN GLASS...BUT YOU'RE ALL RIGHT? YOU FOUND THE SOURCE OF THE DUPLICATES?

THEY WERE SENT BY THE MASTER OF MIRROR-WORLD, IF YOU CAN BELIEVE IT, ***QUEEN NUBIA.***

I MUST HAVE CRASHED THROUGH HIS REALM ON MY WAY BACK TO EARTH. I DIDN'T EVEN REALIZE IT...

I CAN'T HELP BUT FEEL RESPONSIBLE FOR THIS WHOLE MESS.

THIS ISN'T ON YOU--DON'T DO THAT.

WE ***BOTH*** KNOW THAT IS ***NOT*** HOW FATE WORKS.

I KNOW. AND I'M SORRY, I'VE BEEN MEANING TO GET IN TOUCH WITH MOTHER TOO. SHE'S PROBABLY FURIOUS--

YOU'RE APOLOGIZING AGAIN. STOP IT.

BUT YES, HIPPOLYTA ***HAS*** BEEN TRYING TO REACH YOU. MORE THAN THAT, THOUGH, YOU'RE NEEDED ON ***THEMYSCIRA.****

THINGS ARE...

LOOK, I DON'T WANT TO EXPLAIN IT ALL HERE.

SEE* ***NUBIA & THE AMAZONS!* *--BRITTANY*

...JUST COME, AS SOON AS YOU CAN.
I WILL, SISTER.

CHECKMATE UNOFFICIAL TEMPORARY OFFICES, D.C. DIVISION.
CLACKETY CLACKETY CLACKCLACKCLACK
OF COURSE. DANG IT...
BRIIIIINGG BRIIIIINGG

AGENT CANDY--

OH, GURL!
NO-- I'M GOOD, JUST GLAD TO HEAR FROM YOU!

OH, YOU KNOW. ROUTINE CLEANUP.
A TRIP TO THE ISLAND? WELL, AREN'T YOU FANCY.

BETWEEN YOU AND ME, I'VE BEEN PULLING FILES ON CIZKO. HAVEN'T FOUND ANYTHING THAT'LL STICK YET. THAT BOY IS SLIPPERY--

OF COURSE. DON'T WORRY ABOUT SIGGY--HE'S BEING WELL LOOKED AFTER.
AS A MATTER OF FACT, STEVE IS VISITING HIM THIS AFTERNOON! NOW GO, GET OUT OF HERE. ENJOY YOUR TIME WITH FAMILY...

...AND CALL ME WHEN YOU GET BACK!

ELSEWHERE.
NO MATTER HOW YOU CUT THE CARDS, UNLESS IT'S GIMMICKED YOU'LL GET A UNIQUE DEAL.

EVEN IF YOU TRY TO GAME THE DECK, A SHUFFLE WILL SOW *DISCORD* INTO THE MIX--CHAOS THAT CANNOT BE PREDICTED OR ACCOUNTED FOR.

SOME PEOPLE HAVE THAT RARE COMBINATION OF LUCK AND INTUITION--THEY'LL PULL A GOOD CARD *DESPITE* THE ODDS.
10
J
Q
K
A

AND THEN THERE ARE PEOPLE LIKE *ME.*
THE ONES WHO DON'T EVEN WANT TO *PLAY* THE GAME.

I DON'T NEED WINS-- I NEED TO *BE SEEN.* GAIN OR LOSS, IT DOESN'T MATTER.

MY SOURCES TELL ME WONDER WOMAN IS GOING AWAY ON A BIT OF A TRIP...
I SAY, LET THEM PLAY ON THEIR LITTLE ISLAND.
IT GIVES US TIME TO PLAN OUR ATTACK, AND SCORE SOME POINTS WITH MANAGEMENT.
WHICH BRINGS ME TO WHY I'VE CALLED YOU ALL HERE TODAY.
FELLOW MESMERISTS, ALLOW ME TO INTRODUCE MY BEAUTIFUL ASSISTANT...
SAY HELLO, SWEETHEART.
HELLO, GENTLEMEN!
NOW, LET'S GET DOWN TO BUSINESS. THE FIRST ORDER OF THE NEW
VILLAINY INC.?
WHY, WE'RE GOING TO KILL WONDER WOMAN!
TO BE CONTINUED IN TRIAL OF THE AMAZONS

ALTUUM

Altuum concept art
by ANDY MacDONALD

Image-Maker concept art
by MICHAEL W. CONRAD